Vision

Harvard Students
Look Ahead

We dedicate this book to the future of the class of 1993.

Vision - Harvard Students Look Ahead
Copyright, 1993 by Isaac Devash, Sherry Leigh Coutu,
Allison Hughes, Jeremy Verba, and Gary Mueller

"The Genetics Challenge to Society: Moral Issues of the Medical Revolution"
Copyright, 1993, by Joshua Sharfstein

"The Pulse of Change"
Copyright, 1993, by Andrew Reisner

"Artificial Life: The Revolution"
Copyright, 1993, by David H. Ardell

"Future Choices for the Individual"
Copyright, 1993, by Gil Lahav

"Moral Challenges of Science in the Twenty-first Century"
Copyright, 1993, by Kate Tulenko

"Social Ethics, Eugenics, and the Human Genome Project"
Copyright, 1993, by Angelina Christella Wong

"Women in the Year 2000 and Beyond: A Collective Vision"
Copyright, 1993, by Hallie Levine

"The Future of Energy"
Copyright, 1993, by Gaudenz B. Assenza

"The Age of Externalities"
Copyright, 1993, by Carl Phillips

"Evolution toward Humanistic Economic Systems"
Copyright, 1993, by Shanti Rabindran

"Business Beyond Borders Preserving the Common Good:
The Role of For-Profit and Not-For-Profit Enterprises"
Copyright, 1993, by Ian Rowe

"EL SEÑOR BURBUJAS"
Copyright, 1993, by Mark Taylor

"Religious Pluralism"
Copyright, 1993, by Lisa Kemmerer

"Exotic Terrains: An Architecture for the Landscape of the Future"
Copyright, 1993, by Kristina Hill

"Writing a New Chapter in the History of International Relations"
Copyright, 1993, by Andrew P. N. Erdmann

CONTENTS

INTRODUCTION 5

ACKNOWLEDGMENTS 7

ABOUT THE EDITORS 8

MEDICINE

The Genetics Challenge to Society: Moral Issues of the
    Medical Revolution
    – *Joshua Sharfstein* 11
The Pulse of Change
    – *Andrew Reisner* 17

BIOLOGY

Artificial Life: The Revolution
    – *David H. Ardell*...27

PHILOSOPHY

Future Choices for the Individual
    – *Gil Lahav* 33

SCIENCE

Moral Challenges of Science in the Twenty-first Century
    – *Kate Tulenko*...39

SOCIAL SCIENCES

Social Ethics, Eugenics, and the Human Genome Project
    – *Angelina Christella Wong* 47

WOMEN'S STUDIES

Women in the Year 2000 and Beyond:
    A Collective Vision
    – *Hallie Levine* 59

GOVERNMENT

The Future of Energy
 – *Gaudenz B. Assenza* 67

ECONOMICS

The Age of Externalities
 – *Carl Phillips* 81
Evolution Toward Humanistic Economic Systems
 – *Shanti Rabindran* 89

BUSINESS

Business Beyond Borders
 – *Andrew F. Popell* 99
Preserving the Common Good:The Role of For-Profit and
 Not-For-Profit Enterprises
 – *Ian Rowe* 105

EDUCATION

EL SEÑOR BURBUJAS
 – *Mark Taylor* 113

RELIGION

Religious Pluralism
 – *Lisa Kemmerer* 121

DESIGN

Exotic Terrains: An Architecture for the Landscape
 of the Future
 – *Kristina Hill* 129

HISTORY

Writing a New Chapter in the History of International
 Relations
 – *Andrew P. N. Erdmann* 137

INTRODUCTION

The life spans of many people do not allow them to witness the beginning of a new century; even fewer experience the beginning of a new millennium. Now on the threshold of the twenty-first century, those of us who are about to complete our formal studies at Harvard look with many pairs of eyes at this not-so-distant, but still uncertain future. For some it may be a prospect eliciting great optimism; for others, deep despair. Whatever our philosophical inclination may be, this is a time to think about our future and that of other peoples in our world. If present trends give us any indication of what that future holds in store, we can expect both challenges and opportunities, both discoveries and dilemmas. Many of these are discussed in the sixteen essays that make up this book. Representing thirteen different academic fields, the writers are all Harvard students, some in graduate programs, others in undergraduate ones. Their charge is to speak about what they believe our world will look like, from the point of view of their various disciplines.

Although a number of books have been written about the future, this one is unique in that it is structured to bring together students' views from diverse fields in sciences, humanities, and the arts. Each writer submitted an essay without the benefit of reading any of the other contributions, yet it seems at times that they are participating in a dialogue with each other across the pages. Several themes emerge and help to unify both the book and the visions that these authors share.

Whether our futures are predetermined or affected by some accident of nature like the genetic coding or the eruption of a volcano half a world away, these writers agree that to a large extent, the future is a result of our actions today. Prominent in their essays is a call for individual responsibility, the need to become better informed about the complex choices that must be made *now*. The uses to which we put the education that we have received will identify us in the history books that future generations will read.

Whatever the outcomes of our decisions–whether positive or negative, either in the short- or in the long-run–the very opportunity to make choices and accept responsibility is both a burden and a freedom.

The multidisciplinary approach to major questions about the future can help increase our awareness and appreciation of the complexity of these choices. As technology becomes more sophisticated, we ourselves face the challenge of keeping pace, of becoming more conscious of the ethical and moral dilemmas we must confront. This book may suggest some of the important ways in which people from various disciplines can work together to make their vision of the future their reality.

I offer a challenge to future Harvard students to continue the dialogue that these sixteen writers have begun in this first edition of *Vision: Harvard Students Look Ahead*. Future editions surely will expand the efforts of this year's editors, adding more disciplines, responding to themes and questions that these writers have suggested. Such a publication can become a valuable means of communicating our visions to other Harvard students, to alumni, to those who have taught us, and to those who administer the University. Most important, this publication I hope will challenge all of us to think seriously about our future, about what we wish it to be, and then to take charge of making it so.

Isaac Devash
Cambridge, Massachusetts
May 1993

ACKNOWLEDGMENTS

In order to put this publication together, we began an effort across the University to identify writers for the project. We approached the student body at Harvard and, through several channels, asked them to take their specialized knowledge and tell us how it can help us better understand our future and ourselves. Our initiative received an enthusiastic response from both faculty and students, and for this we are most grateful and encouraged.

Bringing such a publication to light required the help of many people. I wish to thank especially the core team of the project, those who accompanied it from its inception to its completion; Sherry Coutu, Allison Hughes, Gary Mueller, and Jeremy Verba. I wish all the success to Allison and Gary, who will be staying at Harvard next year and continuing this project.

A special thanks goes to Emeritus Professor Paul Lawrence of the Harvard Business School for agreeing to take part in the essay selection process. In addition, the core team would like to thank Harvard President Neil L. Rudenstine, and faculty and administration members: Joseph L. Badaracco, Rena Clark, Jerry R. Green, Jay W. Lorsch, Bailey Mason, Dean John H. McArthur, Howard Stevenson, and Jeffrey Timmons for their encouragement and advice.

Many students have volunteered their time and energies at different points in the publication process: Chen Barir, Christian Brix-Hansen, John C. Cestar, Mihir A. Desai, Eytan Glazer, Hani J. Habbas, Edward G. Mallinckrodt, Scott G. Richter, Lisa M. Roseff, Yesha Sivan, Saba Hapte-Selassie, and Tanya Selvaratnam.

I also want to thank our dedicated copy editor, G. Patton Wright of Cambridge Wordwright, for his efforts in the editorial work that occupied many hours.

I want to thank Janet Kimball, at Harvard Business School Press, for her professionalism in guiding this project through to printed form. Special thanks to Susan Manning and Robert Simons for their visionary cover design, book design, and typography.

Finally, I am very grateful to Dirk E. Ziff; the Harvard Business School; the International Students' Committee; Andersen Consulting's Strategic Services Practice; Thomas Kosmos, president of the Mentor Group; and Coopers & Lybrand, for their financial support, without which this book would still be a mere idea in my head.

ABOUT THE EDITORS

EDITOR:

ISAAC DEVASH: Currently finishing his second year at Harvard Business School, he graduated *Summa Cum Laude* from the Wharton School, worked for Credit Suisse First Boston in New York, London, and Tokyo, worked for a consulting firm in South America, and served for four years as an officer in the Israeli Defense Force.

ASSISTANT EDITORS:

SHERRY LEIGH COUTU: Currently finishing her second year at Harvard Business School, Sherry is president of the European Club, member of the HBS women's rowing team, and member of the HBS Show lighting crew. Prior to arriving at HBS, she graduated at the top of her class from the University of British Columbia's Honors Political Science program and the London School of Economics' MSe. Economics program, worked as a management consultant in England for several years and set up a small company. Her hobbies include international travel and outdoor sports.

ALLISON HUGHES: Currently a Junior at Harvard and Radcliffe Colleges studying economics, Allison founded the U.S. office for the St. Gallen International Management Symposium and serves as President of the Harvard-St. Gallen International Business Club. In addition, she is an executive board member of the Women's Leadership Project, the Co-President of the Women in Economics and Government Club, Advisor for the Radcliffe Mentor Program, and Publisher of the Harvard Political Review.

JEREMY VERBA: Currently finishing his second year at Harvard Business School, Jeremy is the chairman of the HBS show and a founding member of the Communications Industry Club. Prior to arriving at Harvard, Jeremy graduated from the architecture program at MIT, worked as a realestate developer in Canada and as a banker in New York.

GARY MUELLER: Currently in his first year at the Business School. Gary is news editor of the *Harbus News* and an active member of the Eastern European Club. Prior to arriving at HBS, Gary graduated from Harvard College, won a Fulbright Scholarship to study in Germany for two years, and worked for two years on political and economic reforms in the former Soviet Union with the Strengthening Democratic Institutions Project at Harvard.

VIEWS FROM

MEDICINE

THE GENETICS CHALLENGE TO SOCIETY:
MORAL ISSUES OF THE MEDICAL REVOLUTION

– JOSHUA SHARFSTEIN

Y ou wake up feeling awful—pounding headache, runny nose, sore throat, the works. You decide to go to the doctor, but today, there's no need for the old-fashioned ritual of physical exam, throat culture, and blood test. Today, all you have to do is spit twice in a plastic bag.

A lab technician tests your saliva for the unique DNA markers of the 200 most common viral and bacterial pathogens. An hour later the results are in: you have a staphylococcal bacterial infection. But there's good news: the bug doesn't carry an antibiotic resistance gene, so that a single megadose of penicillin (given through the ear) will do the trick.

As you leave the lab, the doctor calls you into her office. Your saliva contained a few of your cheek cells, she explains, which were tested for a variety of genetic disorders. One came up positive: your fifth chromosome contains a flawed gene that makes you highly susceptible to colon cancer. You are seized with fear as the doctor says your risk of developing a tumor by age sixty is several hundred times greater than the average person's.

Fortunately, the doctor continues, the government is now distributing a new pill to reduce your cancer risk dramatically. What's more, the pill will save society millions of dollars by preventing thousands of cases of colon cancer nationwide. You leave the doctor's office feeling healthier for the moment and very

Joshua Sharfstein *served as editorial chair of the* Harvard Crimson. *After graduation in 1991 from Harvard College with a concentration in social studies, he spent a year in Central America on a Sheldon Fellowship working on child health projects in Quetzaltenango, Guatemala, and San José, Costa Rica. Last year he began studies at Harvard Medical School. He has written essays for* The New Physician *and* American Medical News, *as well as a series of "Letters from Medical School" published in* Public Citizen Health Letter.

relieved that you have just dodged a bullet in your future.

Sound incredible? The revolution in molecular biology has made the technology described above not only possible, but probable within the coming decades. In about ten years genetics has already conquered diseases that took centuries even to name. In recent months, the genes responsible for Huntington's Disease, Amyetrophic Lateral Sclerosis, and several forms of cancer have been discovered, paving the way for revolutionary new therapies. The pace will only quicken, until eventually, the Human Genome Project will uncover all of the genetic building blocks of the human race and its diseases.

Listen to the scientists responsible for this wave of discoveries and you will hear that the medicine of the future will be cheaper and more effective than ever before.

On the other hand . . .

You are expecting your first child. A routine genetic test of a few fetal blood cells that found their way through the placenta into your own blood reveals a mutation in a key fetal developmental gene. "This could be very serious," your doctor tells you. "Or it could be nothing."

Well, that's a helpful assessment, you think. Then you ask: "Could this have been caused by one of those eight pills you prescribed for me to reduce my future cancer risk? I read somewhere that they were never tested sufficiently."

"Don't be silly," the doctor responds, patting your shoulder and smiling. "It was probably just a random genetic mutation." Then he stops smiling: "I recommend immediate exploratory laporoscopic fetal surgery. By inserting a small scope under your umbilicus, we can survey the developmental damage and, if necessary, remove a small group of cells, transfect them with a normal copy of the gene, and return the cells to foster normal development."

Insurance covers the operation, he informs you, and you reluctantly agree. As you are wheeled to your room to prepare for surgery, you think about how many of the millions of impoverished mothers and children in the world could be fed today with the money for your operation—about a thousand, you decide. Is it worth it?

On your bed is a bouquet of flowers. "Thinking of you," the printed card says and underneath is a handwritten note from your boss: "Having reviewed the genetic test results of your future son, we have determined that your family is too much of a genetic risk for our group insurance policy. Best of luck in your job search."

As with the first scenario, the technology for this prepartum nightmare is not that far away. And it isn't too hard to imagine such a misuse of diagnostic tests and pharmaceuticals. After all, in 1993, thousands of patients receive dangerous prescription medications they do not need. Thousands more are denied health coverage because of conditions ranging from diabetes to angina.

But today's problems don't necessarily doom the future to repeat them. Will medicine lead society to better health and rationality or to greater inequality and rationing? The answer to this question is that medicine will not lead society anywhere. Society will lead medicine. But where it will lead will depend on how we confront—or fail to confront—two critical social questions. These questions have been with us for centuries and have little to do with genes, chromosomes, or deoxyribonucleic acid. Yet the vast technological change that these terms signify has made these questions unavoidable. How the world addresses them will determine medicine's fate in the future and indeed, much of the future itself.

ARE WE EQUAL CITIZENS OR NOT?

Ask people today about inequality and they will probably tell you about injustice based on race, gender, class, sexual orientation, or religion. Perhaps they'll mention the oppression of blacks in South Africa, the virtual enslavement of women in some Arab countries, the genocide against Muslims in Bosnia, or the homophobia that covers much of the globe. Those who object to these atrocities have specific goals in mind. And those who defend them often are defending a long defined tradition of power and privilege.

In the future, however, the neat battle lines of inequality will be broken because everybody, in one way or another, will have a genetic vulnerability, possibly causing everyone to be discriminated against. Do you have a poor complement of math genes? Off to a subpar school! Do you have a gene for asocial behavior? Then let the police track your every move.

Society may well decide to limit health care expenditures for the genetically impaired. And that's a class anyone—no matter the race, class, or religion—might qualify for. In developing countries, such rationing may turn into de facto genocide as diseased populations are allowed to perish.

As genetic differences between established groups are used to legitimate discrimination, genetics may also intensify current battles. Will some try to use gene therapy to turn black individuals white or make gay persons heterosexual? The potential for genetics to undermine the already precarious position of marginalized groups in society cannot be understated.

Yet these risks are not absolute. While medicine will expose all of our flaws, at least it will show us that we *all* have flaws, and maybe we will begin to realize the absurdity of using them against each other. Our shared vulnerability will serve as a common ground that has never existed before. And this common ground may force us to realize that if we do not embrace the principle of equality, all of us will be vulnerable.

Similarly, we all must either secure the right to privacy—or abandon it altogether. As more and more data become available on us, the potential for abuse will increase astronomically. Imagine a manufacturer mailing alcohol to people who have a predisposition to a drinking disorder. Or a retailer storming into your house demanding you buy something simply because your genes showed you respond poorly to intimidation. Will health insurance become known as something available only to the genetically perfect among us?

These issues defy classifications of race, gender, or sexual orientation. Again, a new common vulnerability may create a common base for progress. In the future, equality will either be a mindless Orwellian slogan (Equality—for all equal genetic individuals!) or a rallying cry, as it has never been sounded before.

WHAT IS HEALTH?

Despite the annual United States health budget of over $800 billion, residents spend billions more on traditional therapies. In other parts of the world, traditional healers dominate the medical world. The reason for this is no mystery: modern technological medicine treats the disease more than it promotes health. Traditional healers have long acted under the assumption that the biological basis of suffering is limited and that any successful treatment must address social and psychological issues as well.

DNA analysis will actually prove that assumption correct. Even as genes are discovered for particular diseases, the correlation between the genetics and the disease will often not be 100 percent. That is, not everyone with a poor set of genes has the problem scientists would expect. What is responsible for these persons' suffering falls out of the realm of genetics and, for some patients, out of the realm of medicine altogether. It is ironic that at the same time molecular medicine proves its worth, it also exposes its own limitations.

But how will societies respond to these limitations? We can either deny them or embrace them.

Denial will carry a large cost. In this scenario, governments around the world will invest billions to find biomedical causes of diseases not related to genetics. Yet the world will continue willfully to neglect the real causes of suffering—malnourishment, poor housing, and social marginalization—that could be addressed at less cost. Patients young and old, rich and poor, will become increasingly disillusioned with medicine's unwillingness to see them as people. Doctors will virtually all be specialists in one genetic disorder or another—a model for the medical profession supported by some today. The continued abuse of pharmaceuticals and ineffective technology will guarantee the United States an ineffective health care system with a cost unparalleled in the world. No doubt, inequality will mount under such a system, with expensive new technologies accessible only to the wealthiest individuals.

An alternative future will use the limits of biomedicine to its advantage. As genetics conquers the limited medical aspect of diseases, society will find itself energized with optimism about ending the social scourges that have long plagued civilizations. And where genetics leaves off, society will address the social contributors to disease. A concerted campaign against all causes of infectious diseases—such as poor water, inadequate housing, and hunger—may be launched. Cost-benefit analyses (although bemoaned by many today) will actually point the way to social, psychological, or traditional therapies that are more effective than biological remedies. In this scenario, there will be enough primary care physicians around the globe to implement these alternative treatments.

In the best of all worlds, genetics will give us the tools to understand ourselves, but we will not forget that the whole is far more important than the sum of its chromosomes. If health comes to be seen as far more than medical, all of society's decisions will be more likely to respect human dignity. Admittedly, this is idealistic, but in the future, in the face of such dangers, we will need our ideals.

By answering these two fundamental questions, society will lead medicine toward either the first scenario, in which genetics helps to prevent diseases such as colon cancer, or the second, in which every trip to the doctor becomes a spin of the roulette wheel. But how society answers these two questions cannot be predicted. No doubt, *how* will depend on *who* answers these questions.

Today, the decisions on biomedical technology are made by scientists, doctors, board members of large medical and pharmaceutical corporations, and perhaps a few politicians and judges. Many of these people have the best interests of society in mind, but some do not. What is lacking is the participation of the millions of individuals whose rights and safety will be affected by the vast changes in medicine. The first step to this participation is education. While the scientific technologies are complex, the pivotal issues aren't technical or esoteric. They are moral, and their resolution poses one of the most difficult moral challenges for all citizens of the world. ❖

THE PULSE OF CHANGE
– ANDREW REISNER

Medicine shapes contemporary life in two categorical fashions. First, advances in medicine lead to new patterns of human life: presently, the population of industrialized nations is healthy enough that the average citizen lives more than seven decades. This relatively recent alteration of the human condition obviously has had a monumental cultural impact. Second, an advance in medicine amounts to understanding the human being in a new light. The scope of the research may be macroscopic, such as assessing behavior in a population through epidemiology, or it may be microscopic, such as learning the molecular functions of genes. In either case, medicine is a science uniquely integrated with humanity, and therefore developments in medicine inevitably have philosophical impact.

Medicine is young as a science, yet like many other modern disciplines, it has blossomed dramatically. Society is still adapting to the repercussions, and the situation is ever complicated by perpetual development of further medical technology that alters the course of human life and outlook. To predict the future, however, it is essential to understand present trends, the less than satisfactory development of so-called developed nations, and the essential distinctions between the modern world and the world of antiquity.

THE HISTORY

In the days before aerobics, long before phobias of passenger aircraft disasters, before O.S.H.A. and latex condoms and McDonald's so called McLean Sandwich, there lived peoples so intrepid we might think some particularly rousing Hollywood epic had gone to their heads. There were seafarers and fishermen who set sail knowing not all would return; the expeditions repeatedly had half their rosters eliminated by journey's end; wandering tribes voluntarily left sunnier climes to take up lifelong residence in harsh locations prone to winters of long, bleak nights and

---

Andrew Reisner is a first-year medical student at Harvard. He studied biology and mechanical engineering as an undergraduate at Stanford University.

punishing snowstorms. Military conflicts lasted decades, and for such wars several generations of soldiers sharpened their blades and followed their lord's standard-bearer off to distant lands to confront enemies face-to-face.

These characters of history seem to have been so undaunted by danger, their daring so commonplace, it is incomprehensible by modern sensibilities. Yet theirs was an inevitably perilous existence regardless of their bold actions, and this may be the basis of their bravado. The options for humans throughout most of history were grim. Disease and injury threatened humans relentlessly. Of course, cancer and heart disease were obscure dangers: the high mortality rates associated with influenza, diarrhea, and malnutrition preempted the occurrence of most contemporary medical bugbears. Physical labor provided the basis for most livelihoods, yet the safety conditions were medieval, and injuries such as lacerations often led to tetanus or gangrene. Even an agrarian lifestyle must have been perilous, and a life of high adventure perhaps had its own special attractions.

Today's industrialized world is not without its physical hazards. However, most citizens assume they will live to be geriatrics, thanks to a panoply of technological and sociopolitical advances, from antibiotics to modern law enforcement. The safety of the contemporary human condition is unparalleled by that of any other era of history, a liberation from ages of tenuous survival. The frightening side to life is simply less so today. No longer are entire communities of friends and relatives and neighbors obliterated by a season of extreme weather, no longer does every mother bearing a child wonder if she will live to nurse her infant. Furthermore, with each passing year, life expectancies increase. The survival rates for the seriously ill improve, and the length of the twilight geriatric years is extended with improvements in medical science. The benefits of modern life are by no means evenly distributed throughout the society. Yet even in a ghetto, a citizen has a roof overhead, a supermarket nearby offering a selection of hundreds of foodstuffs, and perhaps even a television or a stereo in the living room. Only the nation's homeless and unemployed seem fundamentally to be deprived of what may be called the modern condition, though shelters and welfare programs were not available to the majority of vagrants who once roamed the earth.

THE SYMPTOMS

Like the miserly nouveaux riches, freed from the toil of making ends meet yet obsessed with financial security, many people today who no longer need to struggle to survive remain preoccupied with their health and longevity. Those obsessed with their mortality count and recount, not some trove of gold coins and stocks and bonds, but rather their years left according to actuarial tables. Birthdays dismay the modern adult. The completion of each decade—the 20s, the 40s—is a milestone on a dead-end road. Others are less deliberative of their life course, yet appear unenthusiastic of what should be their unprecedented peace of mind. Working class or upper class, some of them spend their years nihilistically, drinking heavily, or viewing hours of sit-coms, or even abusing drugs. The allure of escapism is easily explained for those in perilous straits, as a way to put terror to rest, if just temporarily. However, with respect to those not living in immediate danger, it is more complicated to explain from what it is that they wish to escape. These issues are germane to the physicians who treat patients including drug addicts and alcoholics. Physicians may grow ambivalent or frustrated if new-found powers to thwart disease merely serve to increase the quantity of their patients' sullen lives.

There are crusaders in this age, and for many their quest is to make the modern world even less perilous. Public interest groups lobby for mandatory seatbelt laws and motorcycle helmet laws; organizations seek charitable donations and fund the researchers who toil away, trying to thwart cancer biochemically; associations sponsor ads graphically illustrating the health consequences of smoking and other vices. All of these efforts are indeed valuable and will cumulatively prevent tragedies. However, the agenda seems lopsided, for as distinct effort is made to extend life for individuals, few crusaders work to take advantage of the security of the modern world. It seems that the increase in life span has created a void, and many fill that void with effort to further increase the human life span. In so many respects, the less terrifying modern world has failed to nurture a more vigorous, more sophisticated society.

The situation is not all bleak. Ethical standards have matured as suddenly as the modern margin of safety expanded. Principles such as equality of opportunity for all have gained popular voice leading to the extension of suffrage and equal rights in this century. Furthermore, the quantity of institutionalized altruism is unprecedented by historical standards. There is some organized effort to improve the quality of life for the underprivileged in this nation and abroad. A powerful contingency in the society is genuinely concerned for the welfare of all humans. These missions lead to a sense of purpose and a degree of self-fulfillment in those involved, and is certainly a positive manner in which to combat the modern existential malaise. However, it would be ironic if the only source of contentment in this luxurious society is to extend the luxury to those deprived of it. This creates a great potential for disaster: prosperity may some day be spread across the globe, obliterating outlets for beneficence.

To write that the human race is on an unfortunate collision course with utopia is a ridiculous overstatement; rather, it is more likely the human psyche has yet to adapt to the developments of the last two centuries. Longevity is now the rule, yet today's combination of human culture and biology are presently ill-equipped to take advantage of the miraculous transformation. In the past, the struggle was well defined for most: to survive and reproduce. Behavior that allowed people to survive and propagate was universally practiced. For thousands of years prior, cultures were predicated on the arduous task of protecting a fragile existence. Along these lines, the prevalent philosophies were not necessarily the most logical and self-consistent; rather, any phi-losophy that offered a psychological edge in the contest for survival was the most common philosophy because its practi-tioners would tend to survive and thus be prevelent people.

An examination of gender roles offers one example of how the modern condition is discontinuous with prior behavior. Tradi-tionally, having the male as the provider and the woman as materfamilias proved a successful propagation strategy, one found around the globe; thus, it may be inferred that traditionally this arrangement led to sustained, vibrant communities able to sustain challenges to survival. The strategy was thus reinforced in the essence of both human culture and ancestral biology. Today, because such roles are not necessary for survival, there is much turmoil in the interplay between new possibilities, antiquated traditions, and underlying biological tendencies. The issues at stake include both the cohesiveness of the modern society as well as self-determination for all citizens regardless of gender. Pres-ently, these two values are seen in opposition with one another. Social conservatives advocate traditional roles as the most promis-ing manner of maintaining social structure, whereas progressives are pressing to attempt a liberated new order. As a result, how women and men should best interact is ambiguous to many young adults, leading to general confusion, anxiety, and resentment.

The magnitude of human competition likewise seems ill-suited to a truly enlightened era. Once attributed to the instinct to survive the oppressive conditions and scarce resources of the past, today's competitiveness persists for other reasons. Some people are driven to acquire ever more, putting in eighty-hour work weeks even when the interest on their personal assets would be a comfortable income. Their rate of drug addiction, divorce, and suicide offer empirical evidence that money does not buy happiness. Despite the availability of housing and ample food and cars and televisions and VCRs, many are consumed with envy and dream of someday being richer. In the modern world, the preoccupation across all strata is with relative wealth, not absolute. Failure makes people miserable yet not everyone can come in first or even be above average.

Medical knowledge itself leads to a reevaluation of many cultural standards and conceptions. As studies show that phenomena from criminality to schizophrenia to religiousness are correlated with various environmental and hereditary factors, free will and personal responsibility are often dismissed: "I don't really know why I can't stop drinking, but I've heard it's genetic." Depression is treated pharmacologically, successfully so in a majority of cases. While this approach to emotional health is considered by many to be a quick fix, or an unsatisfactory resolution, is it that different from providing a diabetic with manufactured insulin? Modern research has suggested an iconoclastic paradigm of the human being as a walking collection of chemical reactions, where emotions and behavior are as physical in nature as the beating of a heart. More detailed medical knowledge has led to great cultural ambivalence. Political wars rage in this society over the meaning of life itself. Is there a cosmic imperative for a little floating organic ball with less cellular complexity than the oft-swatted mosquito to implant itself in the wall of its mother and change her life forever? Does the mother have the right to kill her child once it has eyes and ears and nostrils and fingers and a nervous system, though its lungs mature slowly and it can't live outside her womb yet?

Strategies for Future Management

Most religions fail to address explicitly these pressing contemporary issues. Although direct in how to behave toward parents and spouses and when to pray, little guidance is offered concerning a nuclear energy policy, a genetic engineer's code of conduct, and the structure and spread of representative democracies. The days of living legends have ended, since the effectiveness of the modern media in investigating and broadcasting prohibits any individual from growing larger than life. With foibles present and past so widely heralded, politicians are no longer apotheosized. On the one hand, this reflects a more sophisticated populace, too cynical to deify its merely mortal leaders. On the other, this jaded society becomes unable to unite, unable to be inspired, and it begins to fracture. In short, the modern population may be too well informed to believe in anything.

To recapitulate, the safety of the modern condition both affords the average citizen an extended life span and frees that individual from the daily fretting about survival. The scientific knowledge that serves to extend the average life span also contradicts traditional beliefs in some fashion. Traditions that served to aid communities in their survival now seem arbitrary. From classic gender roles to religions, many standards and conceptions integral to both human culture and biology are popularly perceived as obsolete or incomplete, and the society has hardly had time to do more than adjust through sheer reflex.

Humans need belief systems and will continue to have ambitions to seek for a meaning in life and to provide the motivation to live until tomorrow and guidance with how to spend today. The revelation that philosophies were either arbitrary or false or at least incomplete have challenged the modern populace, which now must strive to adapt to new knowledge. At present, successes are rather limited. For instance, cultural relativism champions the notion that morals and values are the products of cultural and personal predilection. Moral relativists observe that what is viewed as desirable in one society may be egregious in another, yet neither opinion is cosmically mandated. In response, cultural relativists argue that since values are subjective, it is *wrong* to find one culture superior to another. As with homosexual Christians, likewise only partially subscribing to the arbitrary nature of values, confusion and contradiction may be inevitable as humans strive to find meaning in life.

Specific human values cannot be logically validated. Those who cite this notion to attack an ethic they disfavor are tearing out all meaning from human life. Interestingly, both liberals and conservatives advocate self-contradictory values. Conservatives seek social structure based on tradition. This leads to curious moral positions such as that of the Christian fundamentalists who advocate the death penalty and severe limits on welfare. Although they may argue that such policies amount to a pragmatic cruel-to-be-kind sort of strategy, it is *not* the behavior advocated in the New Testament. Progressives stridently condemn the old, arbitrary morality and advocate family structures and codes of conduct liberated from old constraints. Yet prioritizing the acceptance of all nonviolent behaviors and well-intentioned beliefs is itself an utterly arbitrary morality. Moreover, their insurrection against tradition may destroy the social structure rather than refine it. The drive to evolve a society with self-consistent, equitable laws and mores is understandable; yet presently the transition is turbulent.

The changes in human understanding, in life span, in lifestyles, and in biological knowledge have occurred abruptly, and continuity with prior ages is severed. The modern citizen lives with beleaguered belief, for nothing remains wholly trustworthy—not religion, not authority, not even the concepts of the self and free will. There is a minimal connection with the past, and the concern for the future is severely limited. We have less than ever before to dream about and wish for. Yet placing the situation in perspective offers reasons for optimism. These changes have been sudden, and we have scarcely begun to adapt to our good fortunes. If the future holds a world as safe as today's, it may even harbor a populace grown better able to accept challenging new discoveries, a society more sophisticated and balanced, even one more content. ❖

A VIEW FROM

BIOLOGY

ARTIFICIAL LIFE:
THE REVOLUTION

– DAVID H. ARDELL

D o you know why life happens? Traditionally, only religious faith, creation myths, and soupy speculation offered answers to this question. If you open a physics text, you see lots of equations, whereas a biology text, if you're lucky, will give you colorful pictures, but no equations. You can't even find a good definition of what life is. Sometimes you'll read a description—qualified by "most biologists agree"—of what life *does,* but not what it *is* or why it happens. The question is perplexing, given that thermodynamics tells us that matter is supposed to get more disorganized through time, not organize into a dog, get up, and lick you in the face.

It may take twenty years, more likely fifty or a hundred, but we are at the edge of another scientific revolution, one that promises to answer this question and related ones about consciousness and social evolution. Its name is Complexity Science, and it is based on concurrent developments in mathematics, computer science, economics, physics—many of which have happened since we, the graduating class of 1993, began our lives. It is revolutionary by virtue of its methodology. Whereas biology has traditionally operated through an analytical, reductional process of disassembling living things, some tenacious researchers with the advent of powerful computers are building living things from the bottom up: not from carbon-based organic molecules, but from such computer-generated ephemerals as Cellular Automata.

Cellular Automata are simple-minded creatures. They don't move around, so they are forced to "socialize" only with their immediate neighbors. Imagine a checkers board: the Automata

David H. Ardell was born and reared in West Los Angeles. After graduation from Harvard this year with a degree in biology, he plans to return to the West Coast. His interests include acting, cooking, drumming, travel and languages, exploring the outdoors, and the scientific pursuit of our own evolution. He plans to further his studies in graduate school, possibly in applied mathematics, and eventually to join the research efforts of an organization like the Santa Fe Institute.

(the individual squares) are "on" if occupied by a checker—of only one color, for this game has no opponents—and "off" if empty. The rules are not those of checkers but even simpler: each "move" (also called a "generation") consists of each square of the board being turned on or off or staying the same, according to how many of the square's eight neighbors are on after the last move.

The exciting stuff happens after you give a computer an initial grid of "on" checkers to play with and set it going. You, as the researcher, have to look at the big picture. Groups of "on" Automata together with their neighbors form clumps of different shapes. Some shapes annihilate; other never move or change; still others move, retaining their shape despite being composed of different Automata over time, like an everlasting whirlpool in a flowing river, as Professor Terry Deacon once mused. The object stays the same in form, but is constantly composed of different parts. There are also shapes that never stop changing, but continue to evolve, sometimes spewing out copies of themselves into other parts of the grid.

One could say "Bah! Humbug!" to calling such electronic frivolity "life," but there is a community of scientists at the Santa Fe Institute who focus on this system and others like it for exhibiting "emergent" behavior: the whole is greater than the sum of its robotic parts. It is a model for studying why the dance of millions of boring and predictable organic molecules come together to give you Jay Leno. Again, when I say "why" and not "how," I am referring not to the machinations of how this particular Jay Leno came about (Johnny retired), but what this particularly curious property of matter in the universe might be, such that it tends to organize itself into cells, tissues, organs, comedians, societies, and the biosphere.

The Santa Fe Institute comprises four Nobel laureates and hundreds of senior faculty from universities around the world. Among them is Christopher Langton of the Center for Nonlinear Studies at Los Alamos National Laboratory who writes,

> Only when we are able to view *life-as-we-know-it* in the larger context of *life-as-it-could-be* will we really understand the nature of the beast. Artificial Life (AL) is a relatively new field employing a *synthetic* approach to the study of *life-as-it-could-be*. It views life as a property of the *organization* of matter, rather than a property of matter which is so organized. (2)

Life does not have to be mediated by organic molecules to be "life," much as stories do not have to mediated by books to be stories; it is the peculiar mix of redundancy and information in the way the medium is organized that should be called "life."

Are we prepared for a scientific answer to the question of why we are here? This is dubious, considering that the question's traditional answers, often concerning souls and such, have served to flatter us that we are more than merely spawn of the mundane world that we see around us. Will we let Cellular Automata finish the job that Galileo and Darwin started, booting us from the universe's center stage without even a decent concept of free will to distinguish us from the rest of creation? In other words, if the idea of a thinking, living computer scares you, sit down. You just might be one yourself.

The Cartesian premise that human will cannot be mechanical in nature is based on the assumption that the universe itself is *deterministic,* like clockwork. Given enough computational power, this worldview goes, we could use equations like Newton's to describe exactly what the universe will look like at any future instant, given knowledge of its initial conditions. But humanity transcends this predictability, necessitating a divine source for our actions.

But twentieth-century physics holds for us an often unheard lesson: the universe isn't deterministic. Electrons don't orbit nuclei like planets. They jump around and can only be described by probabilities. We have no very precise idea what *any* electron will be doing in the next second, let alone all of them. A generation of physicists struggled with this concept. Even Einstein refused to accept it, proclaiming that "God does not play dice with the universe." Yet today this probabilistic view of the universe is taught in undergraduate science courses.

If the world's most fundamental particles are impossible to predict exactly, should we expect any more of the objects composed of them? Cellular Automata are hard to predict: two similar starting conditions can lead to dramatically different results, and it is usually too difficult to say what will happen to a single starting pattern because there are too many independently acting parts. We are used to paying attention in science to the things that are predictable, that average out, or can be at least statistically described. Perhaps it is time to use our imagination to invent a new mathematics, entertain new assumptions, and continue our progress in uncovering the splendid patterns of creation in the macroscopic world—patterns that underlie how things change and affect each other in ways that are somewhat different each time.

It is time, and the new mathematics is upon us. Have you seen fractals? If you haven't, you need not look far: they adorn many items of popular consumption such as calendars, tee-shirts, and Grateful Dead bumper stickers. These objects, first realized on a computer in 1980 by Benoit Mandelbrot, and the related field of Chaos are at the frontier of solvable equations describing real-world properties called nonlinear dynamics. This mathematics is giving us more exact descriptions of phenomena that change through time: heartbeats, bird positioning in flocks, long-term weather patterns, and the neural firings that underlie the workings of our brains.

Fifty years before Einstein proposed his General Theory of Relativity, the mathematician Georg F. B. Riemann was laughed at for considering what would happen if the angles of a triangle summed to more than 180°. Considered at best a frivolous contribution at that time, the theory has become known today as spherical geometry, and it so happens that it was precisely what Einstein turned to when he needed new mathematics to express his revolutionary ideas.

I am not claiming that the curve of history will repeat itself exactly. That would, in fact, be contrary to my opinion that human societies are themselves complex systems, nondeterministic in nature, and adaptable through learning to all sorts of changes in their world. Perhaps this scientific revolution will be greeted not with fear and outrage, as were many of those of the past, but with the thrill of recognition and amazement. The ideas that might soon issue forth from the mouths of Westerners—ideas about human "spiritual unity" with the universe, about the importance of looking at the whole of things—are not unprecedented in the history of human cultural beliefs, but have been passed on and taught in societies much older than our own.❖

Reference

Langton, Christopher G., ed. *Artificial Life*. Redwood City, California: Addison-Wesley, 1989.

A VIEW FROM

PHILOSOPHY

FUTURE CHOICES FOR THE INDIVIDUAL

– GIL LAHAV

During the past 10,000 years, the human experience has undergone a remarkable evolution as it has been transformed by ideas and the people who articulated and defended them. One of the interesting features of history is that it implies change, and yet leaves ample room for constants; ironically, the more some things change, the more they stay the same. Advances in science and technology will change dramatically the nature and number of choices individuals can make, yet some areas of human ignorance will simultaneously remain unaffected by these advances. While this perpetual state of partial ignorance may be humbling, it also enriches the human experience with marvels, subtleties, and mysteries.

One of the most philosophically profound changes confronting us between now and the turn of the millennium is the tremendous increase in the number of choices available to the individual. These will encompass nearly every sphere of decision-making: the moral, the economic, the social, the political, the cultural, and even the biological. As technologies become increasingly sophisticated and accessible to the general public, they will flood the ordinary person with legions of potential information and knowledge. Knowledge that used to take months of research to assemble will be available within hours. To an ever greater extent, people will have to decide which information they wish to explore and what they intend to do with it.

Gil Lahav is a junior studying philosophy and considering a career in international law and business. When not working on his six classes, developing meaningful friendships or contemplating the cosmos, he participates in various extracurricular activities. He is an editor of the Harvard Crimson *and the* Harvard Review of Philosophy, *and he serves on the Undergraduate Council as the co-chair of the Environmental Affairs Committee.*

With the increased storage capacities of data systems around the world, less information will be discarded. This enhanced ability to preserve information will present the public with various ethical and political problems. How will the privacy of individuals and public officials be maintained, when their every conversation and transaction has the potential to be recorded somewhere? If access to a powerful computer and espionage devices becomes virtually universal, then the consequences of this potential invasiveness may be mitigated only by a kind of Prisoner's Dilemma. If somebody knows something potentially harmful about someone else, then a nexus of blackmail may emerge, such that everyone eventually agrees to mind his or her own business or at least not to divulge sensitive information about others, for fear of retaliation.

Discoveries in genetics will present people with further complex ethical choices. Humans will have to decide the extent to which they wish to meddle in what was once left, depending on one's beliefs, to biological probability, nature, or the divine. Soon people will be able to select the kind of offspring they will produce, from hair color to psychological disposition. These kinds of choices will themselves reflect larger questions about what one values in a human being. The public may have to decide whether and how to insure that some group of scientists does not try to design a breed of genetically superior humans. Advances in genetic engineering may create a realm of biological choices and problems that before existed only in science fiction.

Reflecting on the future can often be a heady and exciting exercise. As humans become increasingly capable of achieving their Promethean goals of knowing, making, and doing everything, they sometimes can wax vain and even reckless. So in speculating about the power, genius, and problems of humanity in the near future, it is also important to remember that humans are just what they are: only human. It is the limitations that are the concomitants of this fact that preserve a certain (humbling) constant in the human experience. Some of these constants are best understood from the philosophical perspective. Philosophy is probably one of the disciplines most apt to remind us, again and again, of how little we know or understand about the universe.

Science and philosophy have both participated significantly in the evolution of the human experience. While both have often served a common aim, increasing our knowledge of the universe, they have also taught us very different things about the nature of progress. Scientific progress can be made when the collection of empirical data either corroborates or disconfirms hypotheses about the natural laws of the universe. Philosophical progress, however, depends more heavily on justification, and cannot appeal to many collectible facts for definite answers. Thus as scientific questions are answered, many philosophical questions persist, tempering our scientific hubris, and reminding us of just how awe-inspiring the universe can be. The second part of this essay will try to survey some of the areas of knowledge that will probably continue to remain unanswered questions, throughout the near future.

By the end of the millennium, we will still not know the truth about solipsistic skepticism. Is it true, to borrow Hilary Putnam's example, that we are nothing but brains in vats, whose every thought and experience is controlled by mad scientists? Is our visual experience of these very words and their meaning being entirely contrived by someone who controls our minds? Do our experiences at all correspond to reality? There will probably not be definitive answers to these queries any time soon, but this kind of ignorance will probably not change our lives much. Consequently, we may decide to deny that such questions have any coherence or practical import.

Other metaphysical investigations will continue to linger and inspire wonder in humanity. While advances in physics and the other sciences may provide us with a more enriched understanding of the nature of reality, we will still not know why there even is a reality. We will still be able ask why the universe even exists in the first place, and why, of all the possible universes that could exist, this is the one that does exist. To these questions there may never be answers. This is partly because, in explaining why or how the universe (in its entirety) came to be in the first place, one would need to appeal to something outside of the universe, and then the origins of that something would need to be explained.

Certain queries about the past and the future will never have answers. Regardless of how technologically advanced we get, we will never know the truth about counterfactuals. For example, what would the world be like today if John F. Kennedy had not been assassinated? It is unlikely that any scientific knowledge will enable us to answer such a question about the past. Consequently, historians and social scientists will always be able to debate and analyze the various historical roles and contributions of past people and events.

Similarly, the future of human action may always have to remain a mystery, independently of scientific progress. The freedom of human agency is logically dependent on this ignorance. If Bob, for example, correctly and certainly knows that Jane will fly to China tomorrow, then Jane no longer has the freedom not to fly to China tomorrow. Therefore, as long as Jane is to retain her freedom with respect to what she does tomorrow, Bob cannot correctly and certainly know what she will do tomorrow.

If science ever does reveal a completely deterministic picture of the universe, in which every future action and event can be precisely predicted, then human agency would disappear. Consequently, people could no longer be held responsible for their actions—since their actions would be determined—and then morality and justice would no longer be concepts that are relevant to the sphere of human conduct.

The unlikelihood of science soon uncovering a perfectly deterministic picture of the world should give some reason for relief. It is hard to imagine how determined lives could have any meaning; if we felt that our lives had any meaning, it would be only because we were determined to feel that way. From a philosophical perspective, our determined lives—our dilemmas, deliberations, thoughts, decisions, and actions—would be just like a collection of billiard balls whose every movement is dictated entirely by the laws of physics.

On a practical level, there are many profound moral and political questions that will probably remain unresolved in the near future. It is doubtful, for example, that future humans, all of their intellectual and scientific advances notwithstanding, will have figured out how to live together without bloody conflicts and without large populations starving to death. It is also unlikely that any universal consensus will be reached about the best political and economic system by which to organize human societies. It is also fairly improbable that questions about the value of life, in its various stages and deviations, will be solved; euthanasia, abortion, and the death penalty will probably continue to be controversial for many years.

On a more fundamental level, the subjectivity of human experience will itself insure that certain questions, debates, and mysteries endure beyond the near future. What is beauty? What is love? As long as humans retain their individualism, there may never be final answers to these questions. In a sense, to define things like beauty and love is to define a part of oneself. Such indeterminacy may be completely desirable; perhaps the most beautiful thing about beauty and love is their intense subjectivity. Perhaps it is only through subjectivity that the human experience will always be filled with mysteries and the wonder they inspire.

The many changes in science and technology that the future will bring promise an ever more complex array of choices and issues. Yet, in spite of these changes and the variables that go along with them, there will still be significant gaps in what we know or are certain of. Many of these gaps are, in a sense, articulated in the perennial, central questions of philosophy. Perhaps, then, humanity might improve its perspective by balancing its confidence in scientific certainty with the certainty that humanity will always contend with uncertainty. ❖

A VIEW FROM

SCIENCE

Moral Challenges of Science in the Twenty-First Century

– Kate Tulenko

I
n his book *The Threat and the Glory*, Nobel Prize winning biologist Sir Peter Medawar warns of the double-edged potential of science:

> It is the great glory as it is also the great threat of science that everything which is in principle possible can be done if the intention to do it is sufficiently resolute. Scientists may exalt in the glory, but in the middle of the twentieth century the reaction of ordinary people is more often to cower at the threat. (15)

Medawar proceeds to discuss the dangers of nuclear warfare, rampant pollution, and the escape of biologically altered organisms. Whereas these scientifically induced physical dangers that dominate the twentieth century will be reduced by the rise of environmentalism and the end of the Cold War, the twenty-first century will be characterized by scientific challenges to our morals.

For generations scientists and philosophers such as Socrates, Galileo, Descartes, Weber, Huxley, and Marx have debated whether science is value-free. A value-free science implies that the source of value is not in nature and science, but in humanity's use of them, whereas a value-laden science is one in which scientific ideas suggest their own use and therefore take on the value of all possible uses. If scientific ideas do have an inherent morality, then inevitably some ideas considered morally wrong should not be known. This view, however, is ultimately dissatisfying because it suggests that there are some facts, some areas of knowledge, that are so threatening to our morality, traditions, and survival that we

Kate Tulenko is a graduating senior concentrating in biochemistry. At Harvard she served as the editor-in-chief of the Harvard Science Review *and the president of Women in Science. She is the recipient of Detur, Goldwater, and ARCS scholarships. Next year she will pursue a Master's in Philosophy of Science at Emmanuel College in Cambridge University on a Herchel-Smith scholarship. Thereafter, she plans to attend Johns Hopkins Medical School in preparation for a career in public policy and international health.*

do not even want to know them. If human beings deny their ability to control the effects of their own ideas, then the final victory of ideas over the human spirit will be declared. While this debate remains unresolved, theoretical and applied science are currently affecting popular culture, creating moral dilemmas for society, and altering the way we view ourselves as moral beings.

The most immediate moral dilemmas that science poses are the complex decisions for which our traditional moral systems provide little direction. As a result of scientific innovations, we have to make decisions that our ancestors never dreamed of making. Turning to moral authorities—whether secular ones like the United States Constitution, or religious ones such as the Bible or the Qur'an—we receive no clear answers. We do not know what Thomas Jefferson would have thought about forcing women who abuse drugs to have Norplant surgically implanted into their arms, or what Jesus would have thought about aborting a child to save a mother's life.

Many of these new dilemmas are simply old problems that science has changed in scale and ease of committing. When *in vitro* fertilization was first introduced to the public in 1978 with the birth of the first test-tube baby, there was concern that traditional concepts of parenthood would be threatened. But when it was understood that because of high costs, this type of fertilization would be performed rarely, it was eventually accepted. Now that more advances have been made and *in vitro* fertilization is covered by many insurance policies and is becoming a more viable option with egg and sperm donation, embryo freezing, and surrogate mothers, people are rethinking their support.

Science compounds old dilemmas by providing us with so much data that a single person is not able to analyze and understand it all before making a decision. Since scientific knowledge grows at an exponential rate, a new type of Hamlet Complex has arisen in which ethicists, like Shakespeare's Hamlet, are so divided by considerations of a dilemma that they are unable to act. Although maximum information is desirable, the problem lies in deciding what relevant matters should be considered. Reluctance or inability to decide is compounded by the realization that additional knowledge discovered in the future could influence the decision. As a result, society is perilously behind in the business of judging new technologies and deciding whether and how we want to use them. Almost unanimously, prominent science and medical ethicists agree that the various fields of ethics are woefully unprepared to confront the new dilemmas.

The growth of scientific knowledge also creates the moral dilemma of rationing medical treatment due to lack of resources or funds. Drug companies estimate that the development and testing of a new drug can cost several million dollars. A single day in an intensive care unit for a heart attack patient or premature baby can cost as much as five thousand dollars. As more expensive technologies become available, hospitals will have to increase rationing both within a single technology and between different technologies. Patients awaiting donor organs undergo a form of rationing, but this results from a shortage of organs, not a shortage of equipment. In the 1960s, hospitals in the United States rationed access to kidney dialysis machines. Patients were chosen for treatment based on age, general health, number of dependents, salary, and position within the community. These criteria proved so morally disturbing that in 1974 Congress through Social Security guaranteed free kidney dialysis to all citizens who needed it. The program now costs the government one billion dollars annually, all for a treatment that does not restore patients to a full and active life. With the anticipated health care reform under the Clinton administration, this cost-ineffective procedure is unlikely to be provided free for all those who need it. The United States may follow the example of England, which has solved the problem of rationing renal dialysis by imposing strict age limits. No one above age sixty-five can receive dialysis.

Rationing between technologies is equally troubling. The best example is the Oregon Health Plan, which ranks treatments according to cost effectiveness. Low-cost, high-benefit treatments such as prenatal care and child immunization outrank such common procedures as appendectomies and treatments for cardiac arrest. Each year the state must determine how much money it can spend on medical care. Using data of past expenses, the state decides to cover some expenses while excluding others. Fluctuations in the health care budget result in a certain treatment being covered one year and not the next.

This impending increase in the rationing of American health care presents the danger of confusing economic and moral reasoning. Technology is usually expensive—manufacturing requires large amounts of raw materials and labor, and using the equipment requires trained technicians and high maintenance costs. For example, the treatment costs of ultra-premature babies and babies with severe birth defects can reach $50,000 within the first few weeks. The cost effectiveness of treating them is very low compared to that of vaccinating healthy children against common childhood diseases. Children with severe birth defects often must spend the rest of their lives in state institutions where, because resources are limited, patients often receive very poor care.

Most severely retarded or deformed infants and adults can experience the world around them and take pleasure in it. As a result of the economic dilemma, it is often proposed that society provide such infants with only comfort care such as nutrition, hydration, and warmth; it should deny life-saving or life-sustaining treatments like surgery, drugs, respirators, and heart monitors. Instead of acknowledging the decision not to treat them as an economic decision (which it obviously is since society would treat them if it had the resources), society tries to convince itself that it is making a moral decision and that their lives are not worth living. Since society thinks it is making a moral decision, it tries to use existing moral codes to justify letting these children die. Finding the moral codes inadequate to justify its economic choice, society changes and corrupts its morals in order to allow it to do what it wants. Sadly, such corrupted definitions of humanness come into play at the two extremes of life—birth and death—when people are most defenseless.

The second major challenge to our morals in the next century is a much more subtle one. The very nature of our morals is threatened with permanent change. Morals are based on human self-perception and definitions of what it means to be human. Science and technology are able to challenge these definitions and consequently our morals.

Traditional definitions of the human involve ephemeral qualities beyond the measure of science, yet science has the power to disrupt them and change how we think of ourselves. Before modern science, religion and myth provided the means to understand the "why" and "how" of human existence. From this spiritual point of view, humans perceive themselves as either made by or related to higher beings. The moral implications of this worldview are logical. If human beings are related to a divinity, then it is wrong or unwise to dishonor or harm them.

But as modern science provided rational, testable explanations of how the universe and planet Earth were made, why it rains, where people come from, and why people die, many people felt they no longer needed to rely on a higher order to explain the world. Lacking empirical data, science cannot answer all our questions to our satisfaction (what happens when a person dies?), but even these questions and their spiritual answers have been trivialized by biochemistry's tendency to reduce human existence to chemical equations. A biochemical view of death involves the halting of a reaction and the establishment of equilibrium. There is nothing intrinsically wrong with scientific theories; they stand up against testing and make predictions that hold true. The problem comes when we confuse our moral views with our scientific theories. If we were to replace moral systems with the field of biochemistry, we could rationalize murder because chemical equations do not appear to have rights. This is why science should provide us only with facts and why we should make decisions with our morals scruples. Morality is the process, whereas science is the tool within that process. The danger comes when we attempt, consciously or unconsciously, to replace the process with the tool. When we replace moral systems with scientific theories, human rights are not respected because data recognizes no intrinsic morality in human existence. Replacing morality with science results in theories such as Social Darwinism, which justifies the exploitation of poor people by teaching that they are poor because they are inferior.

No longer able fully to accept the traditional definitions of humanness because science has reduced humans to their constituent elements, society has turned to scientific definitions. Often narrow and reductionist (such as the biochemical definition of a human as a chemical equation), scientific definitions cannot cover all situations. Instead, a different scientific definition of the human must be created for each new situation. For example, when the goal is to rationalize abortion, the human is often defined as that which can survive outside a mother's womb. It is reasoned that if the life of a fetus is dependent upon a mother's body (and cannot accept the substitution of another body), then it does not live an independent existence and therefore is not fully human. This sets a dangerous precedent of defining dependents as inhuman and threatens the integrity of all dependents: infants, the elderly, and the handicapped. It is also reasoned that because a fetus prior to the third trimester has no meaningful brain activity and feels no pain, an abortion can be justified. Using the criterion of pain sensation as a way of defining what is human compromises the integrity of the comatose, the retarded, and all those who are unable to reason or experience the world in the same way that others do.

Not surprisingly these contrived definitions result in inconsistencies. Whereas a woman can legally abort her six-month-old fetus, a person who kills a pregnant woman (at any stage of gestation) can be charged with double homicide. This paradox implies that the mother's will alone defines the humanity of her fetus and creates yet another narrow definition of humanity. Instead of justifying abortion by using science to deny the fetus its humanness, abortion could be much better rationalized by using traditional moral codes that weigh the rights of the woman against the rights of the fetus.

The conclusion from this is that our society through science has resorted to situational, convenience-based definitions of humanness that allow us to define any group as less than human based on age, race, health, mobility, mental ability, emotional capacity, or burdensomeness to society. While these situational definitions of humanity affect specific groups, some new technologies threaten the integrity of every person. The Human Genome Project is attempting to sequence the entire DNA code, within which lies information on personal risks of heart attacks, Alzheimer's, Parkinson's disease, obesity, or any other condition that has a partial genetic basis (even though the outcome may be affected by the environment). The DNA sequence alone is quite harmless and is of great intellectual interest; however, if society allows insurance companies or employers to screen individuals for genetic tendencies, our concepts of privacy and of individuality are endangered. Although this reality may seem far off, we must recall how outrageous and unnecessary artificial hearts and *in vitro* fertilization and embryo freezing must have seemed only a few years ago.

Already the ideal of what it means to be human and the moral value contained in the mere act of being have been so undercut that Carnegie-Mellon computer science professor Hans Moravec has suggested in his book *Mind Children* that we abandon our biological heritage (that is, bear no more biological offspring) and instead transfer our culture and our very thoughts to computers whose programs are modeled after our own mental processes. In this highly theoretical and serious book, Moravec argues that computers have the advantage of being able to enjoy human culture while abandoning the fragility of human biology.

Technology is a growth industry. Biotechnology, computers, and materials science have or will soon become the basis of many Western economies, so any problems that science and technology present will only be intensified in the future. Society will be increasingly challenged to define what is human, what type of life is worth living, and how we are to treat our fellow human beings.

It could be argued that science is a doubled-edged sword that has advantages and disadvantages; however, if the disadvantages progressively chip away at our humanness, no amount of luxury can make up for its loss. Thus, we need to decide if humanness can evolve, in the same way as we evolved from more primitive forms, or if there are concrete absolutes that we should struggle to maintain. If humanness is an absolute, if there are some moral codes we should never change (such as the taking of a life), then ultimately society should limit technology that poses a threat to our humanity. If not, who knows what will be the ultimate end of this evolution of the spiritual and physical quality of life. We can take charge of our cultural and biological future and determine that there are certain ways in which we do not want to live and realize that there are ways of being estranged from nature, human relationships, and our own biology, so much so that we would no longer recognize ourselves as a human community. Surely these final risks are far in the future; however, the earlier we start to anticipate them, the easier they will be to prevent. ❖

A VIEW FROM

SOCIAL SCIENCES

SOCIAL ETHICS, EUGENICS, AND THE HUMAN GENOME PROJECT

– ANGELINA CHRISTELLA WONG

he Human Genome Project seems like the stuff of which science fiction novels are made, but the multibillion dollar attempt to create a definitive genetic map by sequencing all three billion pairs of nucleotides within the double helix of human DNA is very real. With the techniques already in place, it is simply a matter of time before science fiction becomes science fact. The project's completion will irretrievably alter the world we know. Armed with a complete map of the human genome and emboldened by genetic engineering, we will have the power literally to remake the human race.

That power will reopen the door to eugenics, the science of attempting to improve the human race through genetic manipulation. And this will not be the pseudo science of the late nineteenth and early twentieth centuries, which sought literally to breed better humans; this will be precision genetic engineering at the molecular level. Although Adolf Hitler's use of eugenics in the concentration camps has stained the discipline irrevocably in the modern mind, the Human Genome Project has made eugenics into a very real possibility, one whose societal implications *must* be addressed. Many of those involved in the project and others in

Angelina Christella Wong, Harvard/Radcliffe class of 1996, is a social studies concentrator. Born in San Francisco on April Fool's Day, 1974, she became interested in the Human Genome Project when she began writing a science fiction novel involving a genetically engineered "self-created master-race." She enjoys writing poetry, drawing, sculpting, studying politics, and philosophizing on the nature of life. She thanks her sister Vickki for her input on the world of the novel and is especially grateful to friend and fellow writer Amanda Weinstein for her willingness to discuss this issue.

both the scientific and nonscientific communities have chosen to address the project as a purely scientific venture. This view is both false and dangerous. Anything which will give us the power to remake the human race has implications reaching far beyond the realm of science.

A Brave New World

The combination of a human genetic map with genetic engineering will give us the power to shape future generations, but to what use should we put that power? Almost no one would object to correcting genetic defects, such as a faulty heart valve or a missing limb; this is, after all, merely a therapeutic extension of the prenatal diagnostic screening available today. Engineering physical characteristics is only one small step further. Engineering for physical characteristics seems innocuous enough: what harm is there in allowing people to select blue eyes over brown, or in allowing all of our children to look like movie stars? But even the most innocuous of eugenic choices carries hidden costs.

It is generally accepted that there is no gene for intelligence, but it is also acknowledged that intelligence is genetically linked. Even with the completion of the project, it is doubtful that we will know exactly what genetic combination produces an Einstein, a Mozart, or a Jefferson. We will have the power to engineer physical perfection long before we have the power to select for mental characteristics—if we ever do. We will run the risk of inadvertently destroying mental potential while engineering physical perfection, of engineering away another Einstein or Mozart or Jefferson because the links between the characteristics that make these people what they are and their physical characteristics are unknown and will remain so even after the completion of the Genome Project. A choice of a physical trait can thus be an inadvertent choice against a mental or psychological one; it may be brown eyes that are linked to the gene which caps off the creation of another Einstein. Genetic selection will carry many hidden costs.

Even if it should become possible to engineer physical characteristics without impacting mental ones, the implications will be far reaching. The idea of engineering for and against certain physical traits presupposes that there is some standard that distinguishes desirable traits from undesirable ones. We as a society will need to decide what composes a perfect human being. Who has the right to make that choice? Whose vision of human perfection will determine the shape of the future? Who will determine what is "genetically correct?" In actuality, there is no such thing as *the* human genome; there is a nearly infinite variety of gene sequences which are all equally normal. To paraphrase Karen Lebacqz, this variety is part of what makes the human race what it is. How are we to define what a "normal" genome is?

The whole idea of creating a standard brings in racial issues. Should there be a separate standard for each race—a perfect white, a perfect black, a perfect Asian? Or should all races aspire to one standard? As Daniel J. Kevles has pointed out, people who have attempted to mold the human race have—either consciously like Adolf Hitler or unconsciously like the nineteenth-century eugenicists—tried to remake it in their own image. Those scientists working on the Human Genome Project in the United States are overwhelmingly white. Whites dominate the highest echelons of government as well, and it is the federal government, by way of the Department of Energy, which funds and controls the Project. A genetically engineered America may become—even without conscious effort—a whiter America. A similar danger exists for another minority: homosexuals. As evidence grows that homosexuality is biologically and genetically based, eugenicists will need to ask; is eugenically improved America will be a *straight* America as well?

The creation of a standard of perfection has profound psychological implications for those who will be measured against that standard. We have already seen the power of television to affect people's conceptions of physical perfection; the effects of a genetic standard of perfection would be overwhelming. Even if the standard is not imposed by law, immense social pressures will push people towards it. Those who do not fit the "norm" by manifesting genetic conformity physically will go through life with intense feelings of inadequacy. Our genes are a fundamental part of our identities, and knowing that they are inadequate cannot but foster low self-esteem. There is even the possibility of genetic trends, of entire generations selected according to one standard which in turn select their children according to their own standards. Thus, it will become possible for all of the people born in, say, 2010, who are red-haired and green-eyed, to select for children born in 2045 to have brown hair and brown eyes.

AT WHAT PRICE KNOWLEDGE?

The technology required for genetic engineering is extraordinarily expensive, hardly affordable for everyone; and the use of genetic selection technology will widen and deepen the social and economic chasms that already exist worldwide. The wealthy will be able to pay for "full selection," whereby they can control nearly every characteristic of the unborn child; the middle class will be able to afford "partial selection," the working class perhaps only a "single characteristic selection," whereas the very poor will have no selection at all. The classes will become ever more entrenched in their current positions, as wealthy genetically "perfect" people pay to have genetically perfect children, while the poor remain unable to afford genetic engineering.

The technology's cost might very well limit its application to First World countries. As nonwhites form a disproportionate number of the world's poor and are the principal residents of many of the world's least developed countries, any factor that reinforces the class structure will also encourage the continuation of this imbalance on a global scale. Moreover, it will be all too easy to cross the line from economics-as-cause of lack of genetic improvement to race-as-cause of genetic inferiority. The fact that certain genetic disorders are more common among some races than others–such as lactose intolerance in east Asians—will only lend weight to the prejudice. As stereotypes grow about genetically "inferior" people and their limitations, genetic selection might very well become the only form of social mobility. Furthermore, as well as widening the gaps between the existing classes, neo-eugenics will enable us to create new social classes of people specifically designed for a single task, such as genetically designed soldiers or athletes. One cannot avoid the fact that social engineering goes hand-in-hand with genetic engineering.

The expense involved in applying the project will have enormous psychological implications for the people who are the actual results of those applications. Genetically selected children will be subjected to immense pressure to succeed, almost certain to result in deep psychological scars. If I paid two million dollars—not an unrealistic sum—to create a perfect child, that child had better be perfect. Failure for a genetically selected child will take on a very personal aspect: all of the failure must lie within the *person,* since the body is perfect. To be sure, environmental influences will continue to affect our children's development, but more will be expected of a genetically selected child than of a nongenetically selected child reared in a similar environment. This has already happened among children who are the offspring of the illustrious donors of the Repository for Germinal Choice: the Sperm Bank.

The cost of the application creates yet another issue. After the initial request for government funding for the Human Genome Project had been refused, Nobel laureate Walter Gilbert announced that the biotechnology firm he owned would take on the project—and copyright and license the results. The scientific community reacted with outrage, and Gilbert swiftly abandoned the proposal. But in January 1993, with little if any fanfare, Harvard University was granted a patent for a genetically altered mouse. Although few people realized it at the time or realize it now, that decision created a dangerous precedent. That mouse and all of its descendants are considered the property—with all of the rights that the word "property" implies—of Harvard. Other researchers and institutions will be required to pay royalties if they wish to make use of the Harvard Mouse. If one carries this thinking to its logical and frightening extreme, it will become possible to patent people. Thus, there will be a royalty for each baby genetically altered to display a given characteristic, adding to the cost of creating a genetically selected child. This will further exacerbate the class stratification; only the wealthy will be able to afford the royalties as well as the actual procedure.

The legal questions surrounding the issue of genetic patents are enormously convoluted. Would a person who is the product of genetic selection be required to pay a royalty fee to his or her creators for any children—children who, after all, will carry the effects of their work? Will the payment stop after a few generations or continue indefinitely? Will people be quite literally indebted to their engineers? If genetically altered people are indebted to their creators, then we will have created a class of people who are less than free. Even the plantation owners of the old South had less control over their slaves.

The Highest Cost

The price of applying the knowledge gained from the completion of the Human Genome Project entails far more than mere fiscal expense. Where, exactly, will genetically created people belong in our society? Quite literally made, much like a work of art or a genetically patented mouse, these people will still have claims to certain human rights. Lawmakers could create a legal place for them—but what place will it be? At the top or at the bottom? Will the United States Congress, for instance, legislate for or against genetically altered people? I believe that Congress will never deliberately create an underclass or an overclass of genetically altered people; such an action goes completely against everything our society stands for. But the price that the use of the technology will exact from the fundamental principles governing our society cannot be underestimated. Democracy is founded upon the idea that all people are created equal and thus have a right to have an equal voice in the government. This idea is the foundation of our laws, our governments, and our views of each other. But application of the Human Genome Project will fundamentally alter that idea. For in a quite literal sense, not everyone will be created equal. The precept that all people are created equal and ought to be treated as such will come under greater and greater scrutiny as the first generation of genetically selected children makes its way through school and into adult life. When I said that Congress would not legislate for or against genetically created people, I was speaking of a group of lawmakers who grew up with the idea that all people are created equal. A Congress that grew up knowing that not all people are created equal will be an entirely different story and will no doubt produce entirely different legislation.

Before the project can be applied at all, fundamental questions of civil and human rights must be addressed. We as a society must decide how far we are willing to go in the name of eugenics, how human rights as we know them weigh against the powerful potential of genetic selection. The fact is that *we must perform genetic experiments on human beings.* There is no other way to determine whether all of the mapping we have done is accurate. There are limits to what even the most sophisticated computer and animal models can tell us. The only way to determine exactly how a given alteration in the genetic blueprint will affect human beings is to try it on one. We can't *not* do it if we want to use this information for eugenic purposes; but *can* we do it? *Should* we do it?

The issue of genetic experimentation on human beings will take on an even more disturbing aspect once one brings money into the equation. The process is expensive, and the initial results will be extremely uncertain. We will want the techniques tested on someone else before we risk our own offspring. Experimental subjects will need to be paid—and paid well—for they will literally be giving up a part of themselves and allowing researchers to tamper with it. The monetary incentives will create another class schism, for it would most likely be the economically disadvantaged who would become the experimental subjects and the economically privileged who would reap the benefits of the experiments. A situation could develop wherein the unborn children of low income people are sold to geneticists as subjects in genetic experiments—an abhorrent idea to anyone who believes in fundamental human rights. Herein lies the one legacy of the Hitler years which may be seen as beneficial. Hitler's attempts at medical experiments on human beings left the world with an intense loathing of anything that resembled using humans as test subjects. This loathing may very well act as a natural barrier to the application of the Human Genome Project, unless all experiments are performed on a purely volunteer basis with no monetary compensation beyond repayment of medical expenses.

Providing that—and this is a big provision—experimentation upon humans does become legal, the implications for human rights will be enormous, especially since the genetic alterations will have to be made on people not yet able to give their consent: the unborn. The debates over the relative rights of the parents and the fetus will take on new dimensions. To what extent do parents have a right to tamper with their children's genetic structure? Do they have the right to make eugenic choices that might damage the child if done incorrectly? The abortion debate will look like a summer breeze in the face of the storm raised by this controversy.

What will become of the rights of people who are the products of failed genetic experiments? It is a foregone conclusion that there will be some failures, for there is simply no way that something as complex as human genetic alteration can be done without at least a few mistakes. Who will be legally responsible for these "mistakes" or legally obligated to care for them if they are brain-damaged or otherwise dysfunctional? Should they simply be culled as soon as they are discovered to be defective? Once more the rights of the unborn—if the defect is discovered in the womb—come into play, as do the rights of the handicapped. In a society where physical perfection will be the norm, handicapped people will be intensely stigmatized. Once the project moves beyond the experimental stage, what will become of those genetically altered children who are less than perfect? Will they or their parents have any recourse? Much will ride on whether or not the scientists who perform the actual alterations are legally responsible for the condition of the resulting child. A precedent might be found in the creation of test tube babies, but doctors are not legally responsible for the condition of the children who grow from these embryos. By extrapolation, the scientists who create a genetically altered child will not be held any more accountable. But those scientists would have much greater control over the results of their work than doctors today have over the results of test tube conception. Will greater control mean greater responsibility? The traditional response has been yes.

In Whose Hands the Future?

The issues of human and civil rights naturally lead to the question of the government's role in the application of the Human Genome Project and, beyond that, the more fundamental question of who is to have control of that application. The government? Private industry? The individual? Upon whom can we depend to use that power wisely and with restraint? No matter in whose hands the power ends up, the end result will be the same: someone is going to end up playing God. Someone will literally be reshaping humanity. And we must carefully consider to whom we want to give that power, to whom we want to trust the future of our world.

Beyond the question of who will control the applications of the Human Genome Project nationally is the question of who will control them internationally. The parallels between this situation and the creation of the atom bomb are frightening. In both cases we are dealing with power so great that it is difficult to comprehend, power with implications we barely understand. There is the same element of fear present during the development of the atomic bomb present here: what if someone else gets it first? Already the United States is keeping a close eye on Japan, which has its own Genome Project underway. The United States government desires a biotechnological monopoly, at least in the beginning—just as it desired a monopoly on the atomic bomb. Some national leaders will not hesitate to apply the techniques to their people; they would not pause to consider the weighty questions of ethics that I am raising. The possible elimination of great minds, the ethics of human experimentation—none of it would matter if they felt that genetic selection would move their country up on the international scale.

The United States has by far the most advanced genome project in the world. In all likelihood, we will complete our map first. We who have studied the nuclear revolution will recognize those questions raised by the genetic revolution: What other countries should be allowed to participate in these manipulations? Who has the right to decide? Can we even hope to control who has it, or are we destined to suffer from "genetic proliferation" and a "genetic arms race?"

Straight on Till Morning

Some advocate abandoning the project entirely while it is still in its infant stages. They believe that we as a world are not yet ready for the decisions which the project's completion will force on us, and they hope that future generations will be more able to cope with its implications. The Founding Fathers used the same tactic in dealing with slavery in the Constitution; they left it for future generations. I believe, however, that the project has progressed to the point where it *cannot* be abandoned. Completion is in sight; if the government does not fund the project, there are private firms that will, and if the United States doesn't do it, there are other countries that will. We've expended too much to turn back now. The genie cannot be put back in the bottle.

The world is not yet ready for the applications of Human Genome Project, but the project is as yet in its childhood. We still have time. We must act as a global society to draw a line between what are and are not ethical applications of the Human Genome Project, between what can be done and what should be done. Thus it is vitally important to move this issue out from beneath the cloak of "pure science" and into the realm of public debate. A dialogue must be established, both within and between countries. The United States must avoid the temptation to try for a biotechnical monopoly, as it carries the same danger that a nuclear monopoly does—a threat to other countries, which argue that they must have one of their own. The world does not need to expend immense resources in doing something that should be done only once.

Governments must take on the responsibility of educating people about the limits and dangers of the applications of the Human Genome Project. If people are properly educated, many of the problems of the nuclear revolution can be avoided. People will not be led to believe that genetic alteration holds the key to solving the world's societal problems as they were led to believe that nuclear power was the answer to the world's energy problems. We must educate society on the moral and practical limits of what can be accomplished with the Human Genome Project: there are some things we simply cannot do, and there are others that we simply must not do.

The heading for this concluding section is taken from the final line of *Star Trek VI:* "Second star to the right and straight on till morning." I chose to end with it for two reasons: I am a Trekkie, and I find the *Star Trek* vision of our future a profoundly optimistic one in which the human race has made peace not only with itself but with the multitude of other races. Moreover, I believe that there *is* a morning, that this quest for the human genome can end in light and not in darkness. Our world has progressed to the point where it is possible to find the light, to reap the benefits of the Human Genome Project without succumbing to the darkness painted in this paper—but only if all of us work together. The Human Genome Project and its applications are not wholly evil, and we are not doomed to live out the picture described in this paper. The project has the power to eradicate the genetic diseases that have made so many people miserable, to help us see what genetic factors act to increase our susceptibility to certain diseases and health problems. The dark side of the project and its applications has escaped the public eye for too long. If we hope to make it to the twenty-fourth century, we must begin now to engage in the dialogue that these complex problems deserve. And I believe that we can make it. ❖

References

Kevles, Daniel J. *In the Name of Eugenics: Genetics and the Uses of Human Heredity.* Berkeley: U of California P5, 1985.

Lebacqz, Karen. "Justice and the Human Genome." Weber Memorial Lecture I, Moravian College, Bethlehem, Pennsylvania, 1 April 1993.

A VIEW FROM

WOMEN'S STUDIES

WOMEN IN THE YEAR 2000 AND BEYOND:
A COLLECTIVE VISION

– HALLIE LEVINE

> *For such reasons compact as they are of many memories and emotions— for who shall analyze the complexity of a mind that holds so deep a reservoir of time past within it?—it seems both wrong for us rationally and impossible for us emotionally to fill up your form and join your society . . . . We believe that we can help you most effectively by refusing to join your society; by working for our common ends—justice and equality and liberty for all men and women—outside your society, not within.*

> – Virginia Woolf, *Three Guineas (105–106)*

Virginia Woolf wrote these words in 1938, as the European continent was on the verge of being taken over by a malevolent dictator. A brilliant writer whose undeniably feminist works had shaken up British intellectuals, Woolf viewed the outbreak of World War II as the result of male militarism. Women, she argued, had no place in any male movement, whether it be to champion the goals of peace or of war. The only way women could achieve real peace and justice—and thus equality—was by separating themselves from the established institution of patriarchy and creating a new community for themselves. Instead of

Hallie Levine, *a member of the Harvard/Radcliffe class of 1995, has a dual concentration in English and American literature and in Women's Studies. She plans to focus her studies on Victorian and early twentieth-century writers, particularly Jane Austen, Charlotte Brontë, and Virginia Woolf. Currently editor-in-chief of* Lighthouse, *which serves as a forum at Harvard for discussions of women's issues, she eventually hopes to follow a career in magazine journalism.*

permeating the prestigious universities of Oxford and Cambridge, they would build new schools for women emphasizing anti-militarism. Instead of merely following the footsteps of the men before them as they entered the professional world, women would work not to become wealthy, but to enrich and assist those around them. Then, and only then, would the great principles of "justice and equality and liberty for all men and women" be realized.

An idealistic and progressive vision, no doubt, but one written more than fifty years ago. Today is not the year 1938, but 1993, only seven years away from the year 2000. At first glance, Woolf's claims may seem to have no validity in our modern world. After all, those same institutions of higher learning that closed their doors to women now welcome them into the ranks of both students and professors. Women have entered all spheres of the professional world. Unlike their sisters of the past, they are no longer forced to hide their talents under the cloak of the private sphere. There are women journalists, writers, doctors, and professors. This past year was designated in politics the "Year of the Women," with numerous women candidates running for office. It would be easy—frighteningly easy—to dismiss Woolf's words as antiquated, having no validity in a world that seems finally to have accepted women.

Yet truly how many steps forward have women advanced in the past fifty years? How far will they have advanced, by the year 2000? The following statistics taken from Marilyn French in *The War Against Women* should perhaps be offered as evidence:

- Women perform between two-thirds and three-quarters of the work in the world, producing 45% of the world's food, but receive only ten percent of the world's income and one percent of the world's property (30).

- In nonindustrial or developing countries, women hold about six percent of government posts; in most European nations, they hold five to eleven percent (46–47).

- Women earn less than seventy-five percent of what men earn for doing the same or similar work; they are still sixty percent of the world's illiterates (39).

Moreover, according to Donna Ferrato, in the United States alone, a man beats a woman every twelve seconds. Every day four of these beatings result in the death of the woman (124).

The statistics go on and on. The picture painted is not one of empowerment; it is one of despair. Instead of having gained respect, women appear to have lost it. Globally, women are mutilated, raped, and harassed. Their reproductive rights are taken away from them as states seek to compel women to bear more children or forcibly to prevent them from becoming pregnant through sterilization. For all that we may hail the next decade as a time of great change and mobility for women, it falls flat as empty rhetoric.

For whom is it the "Year of the Woman"? Instead of becoming united together in order to achieve greater equality for *all* women, women have found themselves divided by race, class, nationality, education, and political beliefs. The wealthy, educated American woman finds herself viewing the world through a much different lens than the impoverished woman struggling to rear three children single-handedly on welfare. After all, what can a woman such as Hillary Rodham Clinton and a young girl forced to perform sexual acts in a prison camp in Yugoslavia have in common? They are both women. Is that enough?

If we are truly to achieve peace and equality and justice for all women, it must be enough.

The year 2001 brings with it the start of a new century, and with it, renewed idealism and hope. The previous fifty years were a struggle for women to gain access to the power and privilege that belonged almost exclusively to men; now perhaps it is time for those women who are in power to help their less fortunate sisters. In the United States, the past elections brought an unprecedented number of women into both Congress and the White House: while our presence in the political realm in no way represents our actual numbers, we can begin to make our voices heard. As journalists, lawyers, academics, corporate executives, doctors, even mothers, women can set goals both nationally and globally so that we may truly achieve a more egalitarian society for women by the year 2000. When I envision the future, these are the developments I see:

1. Women will embrace notions of sisterhood and the collective. Without this ideal, none of the above changes can truly take place. In the modern world, a common complaint of feminists is that women, in order to advance, have "masculinized" themselves. Once in power, women get swept up in the workings of traditionally male society, joining patriarchy instead of seeking to alter it. Women such as Golda Meir, Margaret Thatcher, and Benazir Bhutto may be cited as women who have fought their way to the "top," yet how conscious of women's issues did they remain once they achieved their status as leaders? Letty Cottin Pogrebin, a noted Jewish feminist writer, cautions against what she dubs the Golda Meir syndrome, the "widespread belief that any woman can get to the top if she wants to . . . and that the only reason women haven't achieved more success in politics and business is that they don't

want it" (171). As more and more women rise into positions of
power, it is imperative that they hold on to ideals of justice for *all*
women. In *Three Guineas,* Woolf argued that women who enter the
professional realm should use their careers not for the purpose of
advancing themselves, but for helping others (80). Too often
women, in order to survive professionally, find themselves becoming aggressive and competitive, adopting the same values that
oppressed them for so long. In order truly to help one another,
women need to begin challenging the political, economic, and
cultural structures that have for centuries immobilized them.

2. *Women will be guaranteed the right of control over their own bodies.*
Each year, Roe v. Wade moves dangerously closer to becoming
overturned. By the year 2000, women need to be assured that they
have the right to choose a safe and legal abortion. The Freedom
of Choice Act is a start, but lower class women also must be granted
the same right to choose whether or not to terminate their own
pregnancies. Women will fight to remove all attempts to block
access to abortion due to government refusal to pay for abortions
or state stipulations requiring parental or spousal consent. The
struggle for reproductive freedom is a global one. Too often,
governments attempt to use female bodies as instruments of
control. Under the Ceausescu regime in Romania, women were
forced to undergo monthly medical examinations to determine
whether they were pregnant, and abortion was banned in an effort
to create more workers. In the 1980s, countries such as Japan and
Israel offered financial incentives in order to increase childbearing
(French 102–103). The conclusion is clear: women will work
doubly hard, in both the United States and on a global scale, to
eradicate attempts by the state to control women.

3. *More funds and resources will be allocated to combat violence against
women.* The United States has one of the highest rates of rape in the
world. Not only is a woman at risk of being attacked walking alone
at night, but she must be wary of friends and acquaintances as well.
By the year 2000, both men and women should understand that it
is the attacker himself—and not the victim—that should be blamed.
In addition, social scientists estimate that over 1.8 million husbands batter their wives in the United States. As horrendous as that
figure seems, it pales beside countries such as Ecuador, where
eighty percent of all women report having been physically beaten
(French 187). In order to combat this pervasive cycle of violence,
women need to lobby both nationally and abroad to raise public
awareness. A battered woman often remains with her batterer
because she simply has no other alternative. In the future more
funds will be allocated to programs that both shelter and give
assistance to battered women so that they can gain the strength to
rebuild their lives.

4. Development projects will be created internationally to address the needs of women. Almost all African development projects focus on men. Land reform projects transfer land titles to men, excluding women, who produce both the food and goods for trade. These women are the most overworked humans in the world, spending ten to fifteen hours a day at their jobs, yet legally many societies require a woman to be married before she is allowed access to land (French 33–37). Often the husband will spend earnings from the land on himself, neglecting his wife and children. Ironically, the very projects developed to help women and children only serve to entrap them in a cycle of starvation and degradation.

5. In the United States, a national system of day care will become a reality. For many women, children represent the main obstacle to advancement. The majority of women on government assistance do not choose to be there: they are caught in a vicious cycle with no real escape available. How can a woman go to school and hold a job if she must pay $200 a week in child care? In the United States, families of women rearing children alone are 5.5 times more likely to be poor than those with a man present; a family raised by a black woman alone is 10.5 times as likely to be poor as the family of a white man. Critics today may argue that this country cannot afford a system of nationalized day care, but we will eventually come to realize that we can ill afford the billions of dollars spent on welfare year after year that keep women trapped in such a vicious cycle.

6. Legislation designed to protect women against sexual harassment and discrimination will be enacted. Thirty years have passed since the passage of the Equal Pay Act, but discrimination against women still remains. According to an article in *Ms.*, white women fare best, earning sixty-nine percent of white men's wages ("National News" 89). As more and more women get elected to political office and are appointed to prominent and influential positions on the White House staff, they will work to eradicate the gross disparity in wages. In addition, the new women leaders of the twenty-first century will make clear that they will not tolerate the harassment of women that occurs in the government and elsewhere.

7. Negative stereotypes of women as presented by the media and popular culture will be less prevalent. Naomi Wolf, author of *The Beauty Myth*, reports that five to ten percent of all American girls and women each year suffer from eating disorders such as anorexia nervosa and bulimia. Each year, 150,000 women actually die from the disease (182). In an ideal world, such stereotypes of the pencil-thin model will no longer exist. Recently, magazines have begun to emphasize women with well-shaped, muscular bodies instead of Twiggy-like, emaciated figures. Groups like Media Watch that monitor images of women in advertising will continue fighting against depictions of women in the mass media that emphasize stereotypes of women as weak and powerless, and their efforts will produce positive results.

The year 2001 is not merely the advent of a new century; it is the arrival of a new millennium. For too long women have been subordinate to their fathers and husbands, to their sons and brothers. The past four decades have brought revolutionary changes to the lives of many women. Now, more than ever, as women acquire power, they need to view this as a time to reach out to all women, regardless of class, ethnic origin, nationality, or socioeconomic background, and to help one another. The phrase "Sisterhood is global" may be overused, yet it must not be forgotten. With the dawn of a new century, women will keep these three words in mind as they begin to clear new paths for themselves. ❖

References

Ferrato, Donna. *Living with the Enemy.* Aperture Foundation, 1991.

French, Marilyn. *The War Against Women.* New York: Ballantine Books, 1972.

"National News." *Ms. Magazine,* April–May 1993, 89.

Pogrebin, Letty Cottin. *Deborah, Golda, and Me.* New York: Doubleday, 1991.

Wolf, Naomi. *The Beauty Myth.* New York: Anchor Books, 1991.

Woolf, Virginia. *Three Guineas.* New York: Harcourt Brace Jovanovich, 1938.

A View from

Government

THE FUTURE OF ENERGY

– GAUDENZ B. ASSENZA

The age of fossil fuels will not last forever. According to the World Resources Institute, oil resources will be depleted in about forty years, coal reserves in about 390 years, and natural gas in about thirty-five years (*WR 1992–1993*, 149). Yet for two reasons it is likely that fossil fuels will be phased out before these deadlines. First, air pollution and the threat of global warming will require us to stop using fossil fuels before supplies are exhausted. In order to stabilize the climate, we will substantially reduce carbon emissions by reducing energy consumption, increasing energy efficiency, and developing alternative energy sources. Second, three oil crises in the last twenty years have exposed the vulnerability of the global economy and its dependency on political developments in the volatile Middle East. As Christopher Flavin writes, "Not only is the world addicted to cheap oil, but the largest liquor store is in a very dangerous neighborhood" (Flavin and Lenssen 5–6).

Natural gas has been promoted as a cleaner alternative to oil, since it contains less carbon per unit of energy. However, since the greenhouse effect of natural gas is many times stronger than that of carbon dioxide, even a very small leak of natural gas would entirely offset the carbon dioxide reduction benefits (Flavin 22).

Coal is the most abundant but environmentally most damaging of all fossil fuels. According to Flavin, coal contains seventy-five percent more carbon than natural gas per unit of energy produced (22). Moreover, coal is a major contributor to air pollution and acid rain and will, therefore, be phased out as a primary source of energy.

Some people have hailed nuclear energy as a means to slow global

Gaudenz B. Assenza studies at the John F. Kennedy School of Government as a scholar of the Ernst Schmidheiny Foundation. He expects to graduate in 1994 with the degree of Master of Public Administration. He has two degrees in business administration and has worked in Germany, England, and India. He is the author of a book on the future of economics and has published articles in various magazines on political and economic issues. He has lectured on economics in Russia and Mongolia. A version of this article will be published in Issue no. 9 of The Threefold Review *(the Margaret Fuller Corporation, Philmont, New York).*

warming. Others claim that nuclear technologies are uneconomical and dangerous. They see the roughly 500 nuclear plants worldwide as a permanent threat to people living within a distance of hundreds or even thousands of miles. George Woodwell, the director of the Woods Hole Research Center in Massachusetts, states:

> It seems clear that we have given nuclear power a fair trial and its promise falls far short of even the most modest hopes . . . . [P]olitical systems cannot manage [nuclear power]; and although scientists and technologists may have performed admirably, they have not been able to solve the fundamental problem of contamination of an imperfectly run world . . . . Nuclear Power can be systematically and deliberately abandoned as a potential source of power. (Cited in Flavin 73)

Current energy strategies for the future suffer from a lack of vision. The U.S. "National Energy Strategy" (NES) of 1991 proposes only slight modifications to past energy policies such as increased reliance on natural gas and greater use of alternative fuel vehicles. It is, therefore, not surprising that the NES would lead to a twenty-five percent increase in U.S. carbon dioxide levels by the year 2015 (Department of Energy 179). The future of energy, therefore, will be based on two main developments: 1. energy waste will be reduced and energy efficiency improved, and 2. renewable energy sources will be further developed.

IMPROVING ENERGY EFFICIENCY

Increased environmental awareness and rising energy prices will lead more and more people to assess where reductions in energy consumption can be made in their immediate environments. For instance, car owners will ask themselves whether they really need one or several cars; managers of businesses with all-year airconditioning will ponder whether the permanent use of airconditioning devices is necessary. An increasing number of individuals will ask: What do I really need? What is necessary and what is compulsive or excessive consumption? I do not foresee a system whereby a higher authority decides on what people should buy and how much energy they should consume. Rather, more and more individuals will freely assess their needs and refrain from wasteful energy consumption.

In addition to reducing waste of energy, increasing energy efficiency is a promising option. Since 1973, the twenty-one industrial economies belonging to the International Energy Agency (IEA) have reduced their energy consumption per unit of economic output by twenty-four percent (Flavin and Lenssen 16).

The potential for further efficiency gains is huge, particularly also in less developed countries and the formerly Soviet economies. In the short-term future, energy efficiency promises to reduce greenhouse gas emissions. Flavin argues that measures to improve energy efficiency could hold annual emissions at their current level of six billion tons in the year 2010, instead of emitting a projected nine billion tons of carbon (Flavin 23).

Increasing energy efficiency will not lead to a slowdown in the economy. It will be possible to cut energy consumption of industrial nations without detrimental economic effects. Despite economic growth, less developed countries will keep their energy consumption constant thanks to improved energy efficiency. Developing countries will reap economic benefits by promoting small-scale investments in energy efficiency. For example, by investing $7 million in a plant for fluorescent light bulbs, India could save more than 1,500 megawatts of electrical generating capacity, or $2.4 billion otherwise needed for building new power plants (Gadgil et al.). This example shows that prosperity is not dependent on ever increasing energy consumption.

Investments in energy efficiency in private homes, the commercial sector, and the transportation system will increase, since they are very profitable. For instance, a study by the world's largest electric utility, the Companhia Energetica de São Paulo, concluded that an investment of $2 billion in energy efficiency would save $44 billion worth of new generating capacity (Goldemberg et al. 58).

Improving energy efficiency will not be unaffordable for industries and consumers. After years of dragging their feet, U.S. car manufacturers will recognize that they can substantially raise fuel economy standards without becoming less competitive. Already in 1990, when the average new American car used nine liters of gasoline per 100 km., various mass-produced Japanese and European cars used fewer than four liters per 100 km. (*WR 1990–1991*, 26).

Many technologies that radically improve energy efficiency already exist. This means that the efficiency of lightning systems and the fuel efficiency of cars will be raised without further investment in technological research. Homes will become much more energy-efficient by using advanced construction materials, which reduce heat loss through windows, walls, and doors. In Sweden, for example, some houses need only ten percent of the energy required by the average home in the United States (*WR 1990–1991*, 18).

We will mitigate the threat of global warming and reduce dependence on fossil fuel and nuclear energy by raising efficiency standards, and increasing research and development in energy efficiency and conservation. At the very least, existing technologies will find their way into the marketplace.

RENEWABLE ENERGY

Renewable energy sources are abundant. According to a U.S. Department of Energy estimate, the yearly inflow of accessible renewable energy sources is more than 200 times higher than the use of energy. The annual accessible resources of renewable energy exceed the entire reserves of fossil and nuclear fuels by a factor of ten (Flavin and Lenssen 17). Today renewable energy sources account for approximately twenty percent of the world's energy. In some countries like Norway, renewables provide already more than fifty percent of the energy. In the future, renewables will supply a far greater share of energy. Flavin and Lenssen claim that by the year 2030, an equivalent of fifty to seventy percent of current energy use could be met by the following types of renewables (17–18).

• **Biomass**, such as firewood, animal dung, agricultural waste and garbage, currently provides about ten percent of the world's energy. For approximately 2.5 billion people in the developing world, biomass is the primary energy source. A well-known example for the use of biomass is Brazil's alcohol fuels program, which provides over sixty percent of fuels used in cars, trucks, and buses (Flavin 26). Unlike all other forms of renewable energy, biomass can actually contribute to global warming. Unless the wood and paper used for generating energy is taken from forests that are being replanted, the burning of such materials will increase carbon dioxide concentrations in the atmosphere. The use of wood from virgin forests for electricity generation has the most devastating impact on the global climate, releasing more carbon than if coal were used.

• **Wind** is an underused resource. Worldwide, it produces only 1,600 megawatts of electricity, much of which is generated in California and Denmark. By the year 2030, however, wind could provide ten percent of the world's electricity (Flavin 25).

• **Geothermal energy** is provided by the heat emanating from the core of the earth. According to Flavin, geothermal energy provides more than 5,000 megawatts of electricity worldwide, at 4–8¢ per kilowatt-hour (25). In the future, geothermal energy will supply a major portion of many countries' energy needs, since resources are wide-spread. For example, a large portion of Japan's energy needs will be met by using the immense amount of heat beneath the ground.

• **Hydropower** provides approximately a fourth of the world's electricity. In the past, hydroelectricity for developing countries has been generated by large dams that flood vast areas, destroy livelihoods, and increase foreign debt. The future of hydropower lies in small-scale plants, which are more economical than large dams. Small-scale hydropower is a source of job creation and will therefore help stem migration to cities. Moreover, there is no need to import technology and to borrow huge amounts of capital.

• **Solar thermal** systems are a very promising technology. Large mirrored troughs direct sunlight onto steel pipes in which synthetic oil is heated to temperatures of several hundred degrees Celsius. This oil then flows through a heat exchanger that creates steam for a turbine generator. Another concept relies on parabolic dishes that track the sun and reflect the rays onto a small area, where a special device converts heat into electricity.

• **Solar photovoltaics**, unlike solar thermal technologies, convert the sun's rays directly into electricity using semiconductor devices. Despite low research and development budgets, great progress has been made in the 1980s toward reducing the cost, increasing the reliability, and improving the efficiency of solar cells. As technology improves and mass-production starts, photovoltaics will gain further ground. The U.S. Solar Energy Research Institute (SERI) expects photovoltaics to be competitive with other energy sources before the twenty-first century. Within forty to fifty years, photovoltaic systems could, according to SERI, generate over fifty percent of electricity in the United States.

The potential of photovoltaics is huge. Whereas most standard silicon systems have a efficiency of below fifteen percent, experimental modules are capable of converting over twenty-five percent of solar energy into electricity. Very promising are so-called Concentrator Modules, which focus the sun's rays onto small, but extremely efficient photovoltaic cells. Concentrator modules can convert around forty percent of sunlight into electricity. Perhaps the largest potential lies with amorphous cells, which contain only a very fine layer of semiconductor material (much thinner than hair). Amorphous photovoltaic systems have lower efficiencies, but they lend themselves to cheap mass production. These systems will therefore become the main form of solar photovoltaics.

Two problems of solar thermal and photovoltaic systems have been a concern to scientists exploring solar energy. First, sunlight is a very irregular source of energy, since it depends on the day-night rhythm, the weather, and the seasons. Second, the regions with the highest influx of sunlight are not necessarily the regions where the energy is needed. In order to be able to use solar energy whenever and wherever it is needed, a medium of storage needs to be chosen.

Perhaps the best candidate for storing energy is hydrogen, the most abundant element in the universe. Hydrogen is an extremely clean-burning fuel that creates only water vapor and low quantities of nitrogen oxides, and even these low amounts can be virtually eliminated by using special catalytic converters. Moreover, hydrogen is nontoxic, comprises three times as much energy as petroleum per kilogram, and can easily be compressed, stored, and moved around. Scientists have discovered a way to combine the most natural form of energy (solar energy) with the most environmentally sound fuel (hydrogen). The electricity generated by solar thermal and photovoltaic systems can be used to break water into hydrogen and oxygen in electrolytic facilities. Then hydrogen can be used for storing energy, while oxygen can be released into the atmosphere where it helps living organisms to breathe. When hydrogen is burned, water is again created, thus completing the cycle. Unlike fossil and nuclear fuels, hydrogen preserves the balance of the earth, taking water and giving it back, a perfect model for recycling.

Solar hydrogen will become a major energy source in the future. Photovoltaic and solar thermal plants will be built in those regions with the highest influx of sunlight. The designing of a system of solar hydrogen will be an opportunity to phase out fossil fuels. Even for OPEC nations, solar hydrogen offers great possibilities. After the end of the petroleum age, these nations might still be at the forefront of worldwide energy production, if they now invest in renewable energies. The Saudis have already started installing electrolytic facilities powered by solar energy as well as educating a generation of solar scientists and engineers at the University of Riyadh. Indeed, the financial prowess of those nations could greatly speed up the development of a truly sustainable energy system.

Solar hydrogen has great potential and its use is not impractical. First, solar power systems have reached the threshold of economic viability. Second, for a decade cars have been successfully running on hydrogen. Third, transportation of solar hydrogen is not impossible. In Germany, for instance, a 137-mile pipeline for hydrogen has operated since 1940 without complications. Fourth, there is enough arid land for solar plants, land that cannot be used for other purposes. For all these reasons, solar hydrogen may become one of the primary sources of energy in the twenty-first century.

While it is true that a system of solar hydrogen could meet a considerable part of the world's energy needs, it will probably never be the exclusive source of energy. Rather, there will be a wide variety of technologies for using renewables. Which energy sources are used will depend on the regional climate and resource availability. Once a renewable energy system is in place, each region of the world will have its unique mix of energy sources. Northern Europe, for instance, will derive its energy from a combination of biomass, hydropower and wind power, whereas southern Europe, Africa, South Asia, and the Middle East will rely more on solar energy. In large countries like the United States, which span several climate zones, all renewable energies will play significant roles.

Fossil fuels and nuclear energy have created enormous problems for the developing world. Oil shocks pushed poor countries to the brink of collapse. Nuclear power plants have helped to drain foreign exchange reserves and have boosted foreign debt. Will renewable energy sources bring an end to this debacle?

The use of renewable energy sources will expand rapidly in the developing world. Biomass, for example, already meets half the energy needs in many developing countries. Solar collectors are increasingly used for bringing water to boil for cooking and heating purposes, activities that constitute more than half of total energy consumption in the developing world. Beside cooking and heating, solar modules will be increasingly used for running telecommunications devices, powering signaling systems, pumping water for drinking and irrigation, providing lightning, and refrigerating vaccines.

In many remote areas, photovoltaic systems are already the most economical source of electricity. In India, for example, there are now more than 6,000 photovoltaic village systems (Flavin and Lenssen 20). They are affordable and do not require highly skilled labor for installation and maintenance. Small photovoltaic power devices can have a very beneficial impact on sanitation, agriculture, and health.

How much land will renewable energy economies use? Wind and solar power are less land intensive than other electricity generating technologies. While coal uses 3,642 square meters per gigawatt-hour, photovoltaics needs 3,237 square meters and wind only 1,335 (Flavin and Lenssen 47). Photovoltaic systems and wind farms will not occupy excessively large areas of land. Solar collectors, for instance, will be mounted on many rooftops. And since the turbines and service lanes of a wind farm occupy only a fraction of the land, the rest will be used for agriculture.

Renewable energy sources have substantial technological advantages. First, renewable energy systems can be built in all sizes. Consider the example of solar energy. Whether it is solar hydrogen produced on a massive industrial scale or modules that bring electricity to remote areas, solar power systems can meet a wide variety of energy needs. Many photovoltaic systems are still used in small devices such as calculators, watches, and portable phones. Second, losses of energy are negligible when hydrogen is used as a carrier. Energy can be compactly stored and transported in a variety of ways, such as by pipeline, truck, and ship. Third, renewable energy systems are less complicated and generally smaller than nuclear power plants. Therefore, they can be built much quicker, thus enabling electricity providers to adapt to rapidly changing energy needs. A small-scale hydropower plant, for example, can be built within a few months. Fourth, renewable energy technologies are reliable and harmless, thus requiring neither complex security and surveillance systems, nor expensive maintenance. Solar cells, for example, have no moving parts, and there is little possibility that something will go wrong. We conclude that from a technological viewpoint, renewable energy technologies are will become the main source of energy in the twenty-first century. But the question must be asked, "Can we afford it?"

ECONOMICS OF RENEWABLES

Imagine how the world would currently look if all the money spent on nuclear energy had been put into renewable energies. Likely (if not surely) the world's energy problems would be solved. Surely (not only likely) there would be fewer cancer deaths, fewer nations with nuclear weapons, significantly less toxic and radioactive waste, and no decommissioning problems.

No technology has received as much money as nuclear power. The world's existing reactors cost several hundred billion dollars; the annual cost of operating them and constructing new plants amounts to over $50 billion; and the future cost of decommissioning and waste disposal cannot even be accurately calculated. Despite minuscule research budgets, the efficiency of solar technology has improved so much that the price has fallen from over $30 per kilowatt-hour to under 10¢ for most applications. Further improvements in cell efficiency and in production methods will continue to reduce prices. Perhaps the most important impact on prices will be felt once mass production is achieved. Consider how prices of PCs, calculators, and watches collapsed once the stage of automated production had been reached. Photovoltaic systems are very suitable for mass-production, maybe more so than any other energy technology.

Similar to the factories for semiconductors and other mass-produced high technology devices, those for photovoltaic systems will be located in developing countries, preferably close to the place where they will be needed. In thirty or forty years, photovoltaics will supply a major share of global energy needs for probably less than 5¢ per kilowatt-hour. True, some renewable energy systems are not yet cost competitive, yet the most advanced wind power, hydroelectricity, biomass, geothermal, and solar thermal applications can already compete with conventional energy sources, including coal-generated electricity.

If energy prices included the cost of pollution and government subsidies, prices of conventional sources of energy would nearly double. Only by keeping energy prices artificially low—at the cost of the taxpayer—can the myth be sustained that renewable energies are not cost-competitive.

In order to mitigate global warming, we will start looking at how much it would cost to avoid carbon emissions. Clearly, energy efficiency is the most economical way to avoid carbon emissions. Many investments in energy efficiency would even be cheaper than continuing to operate existing coal plants, implying that the cost of avoided carbon emissions is negative, that is, profitable. Nuclear energy carries the steep price of $535 per ton of avoided carbon. Renewable energies like wind and wood power, geothermal, and solar thermal, are much less expensive, ranging from $95 to $180 per ton of avoided carbon (Flavin 26–27). Investments in reducing carbon emissions by accelerating the development of energy efficiency and renewables will become increasingly profitable. A study sponsored by the Canadian government concluded that a cost-effective strategy to reduce carbon emissions would cost $108 billion, but would save $192 billion (Flavin 27).

The transition from fossil fuel and nuclear based energy sources will benefit the economy for many reasons:

- Currently, businesses and consumers have to pay the taxes which subsequently go into nuclear energy.

- Investments in renewable energies require much less capital than investments in nuclear energy, and they generally produce higher and quicker yields.

- The transformation of the energy system will stimulate economic growth. New companies will spring up, existing ones expand. In the short term, there will, of course, be problems of adjustment, which will have to be addressed. The important point to remember is that the kind of growth stimulated by renewable energy will be sustainable and largely non-polluting.

- Renewable technologies are inflation-proof. After the initial investment, the operational cost for a hydropower plant or a solar complex is largely immune to rising prices.

- Stable or steadily declining energy prices will replace the current cycles of boom and bust, fueled by highly volatile oil crises and daily fluctuations in the world oil market.

Industries like nuclear power generation and oil refineries are extremely capital-intensive, but contribute little to employment. For example, for one million dollars of investment, the oil and gas industry in Alberta (Canada) creates only 1.4 jobs, whereas services generate 32 jobs for the same amount of money (Flavin and Lenssen 40).

In the United States, employment in industries of coal mining, gas, and nuclear power will continue to decline. The creation of a sustainable energy economy will halt this trend of job losses. A study by the Council on Economic Priorities concluded that investments in energy efficiency and solar systems will generate twice as much employment as investments in conventional energy industries (Flavin and Lenssen 41). A renewal of the energy system will not only create new industries and increase the job base, but also boost several professions. There will be demand for wind prospectors, photovoltaic scientists, solar architects, and biomass engineers. Many of the people currently employed in traditional energy industries will still be needed; others will be retrained. For instance, geologists and oil-well crews currently working to extract petroleum could be employed by companies in the geothermal industry.

A new energy system will provide safer and cleaner work environments. Workers and plant operators will not be exposed to radioactivity and nobody will have to decommission hazardous nuclear power plants. At hydrogen stations (replacing gas stations), attendants will not be exposed to toxic fumes and other hazards. Increased safety and more jobs will constitute two important steps towards a sustainable society.

OBSTACLES TO A SOLAR ECONOMY

Anyone who seriously studies alternative energy systems is left wondering why the great transition toward more sustainable sources of energy has not already happened. Here are some of the reasons which so far have prevented the beginning of a new age.

1. Conventional energy industries receive massive subsidies. In 1984 alone, the U.S. government paid more than $44 billion to energy industries. More recently, President Bush, under pressure from the vested interests of energy businesses, granted a $2.5 billion extra tax reduction to the U.S. oil and gas industry (Flavin and Lenssen 27). In the future, there will be fewer subsidies for energy industries, mainly because of crumbling public finances.

2. Today's energy prices do not reflect the true social, environmental, health, and security costs. For example, U.S. air pollution from cars increases health care costs by $40 billion, yet not one dollar of this cost is included in fuel prices. If environmental costs were included, oil would have to be priced fifty percent higher, and coal-generated electricity would have to be twice as expensive as it now is (Flavin and Lenssen 28). In the future, we will rely on the "polluter pays" principle, which will accelerate the development of alternative energy sources.

3. Current energy prices do not include security costs either. If the costs for U.S. preparations for war in the Persian Gulf (even before sending the troops) were included in the oil price, each barrel of oil would have been $60 more expensive (Flavin and Lenssen 27–28). In the future, security costs will be factored into energy prices.

4. Current energy prices are much too low. The low price of

gasoline, for example, is an incentive to waste energy. Moreover, it increases the federal deficit and leads to a lack of competitiveness with European and Japanese cars that have a higher fuel economy ratio.

5. A study sponsored by the U.S. Department of Energy concludes that the first commercial nuclear fusion reactor would not go on-line before the year 2040. Yet more money is put into fusion research than into the entire range of renewable energies and efficiency. Similarly, $5 billion are scheduled for "clean coal" technologies, even though they largely fail to reduce carbon dioxide emissions (Flavin and Lenssen 36–37).

Developing countries have their unique problems of funding the most cost-effective energy sources. India, for example, spends less than one percent of its energy budget on renewable energies, even though they contribute forty percent to the country's energy consumption (Flavin and Lenssen 36).

The investments for efficiency improvements and renewable energy sources were cut in the 1980s. This trend will be reversed as environmental, security, and public health concerns move up the public agenda. The World Bank, which currently provides little money for renewables except hydropower, will become a major source of finance for renewable energies. Renewable energy industries will gain political clout, an increasingly influential lobby, and a U.N. body for its advancement comparable to the IAEA for nuclear energy. Renewable energy departments will become common in universities and renewable energy research institutions will proliferate. Solar physics will become a prestigious academic discipline, attracting the best minds in many countries.

ENERGY STRATEGIES FOR THE FUTURE

Some people argue that we must massively expand nuclear programs, if we want to prevent global warming. Others counter that we must promote clean coal and natural gas, both of which increase concentrations of greenhouse gases. Such policies reflect the short-term thinking prevalent in modern politics. I believe that after intense public debate, most people will opt to build a safe, clean, and sustainable energy system based on reducing waste, improving energy efficiency, and promoting renewable energy technologies. This approach will not require the multibillion-dollar programs now supporting the old energy technologies. By removing unfair rules and subsidies, we will go a long way toward allowing a sustainable energy economy to unfold.

Solar energy is for everyone. No country is without it. The sun is free and abundant; the technology for storing energy, solar hydrogen, is available and proven. Renewable energy sources are clean, inherently safe, and dependable. Renewable energies create virtually no pollutants, no radioactivity, no nuclear waste. They do not require concrete containments and leave no lethal inheritance for future generations. Renewable energies do not cause cancer; they do not require a police state or the limitation of civil rights; they do not leave behind dangerous tombs (nuclear waste burial sites). Renewables do not give dictators the means for the nuclear bomb. Terrorists have no interest in them either. Renewables do not increase the federal deficit, weaken the balance of payment, deplete foreign exchange reserves, increase debt for developing countries, or create dependence on foreign resources. Renewables do not cause acid rain, air pollution, or global warming.

Renewables deliver energy that is abundant, clean, and sustainable. Alternative energy technologies are already economically competitive and prices will continue to drop. Renewable energy technologies are friendly both to human beings and to nature. They will help countries keep their pledges to reduce carbon emissions. For the developing world, renewables are an opportunity to save billions of dollars and to follow a sustainable energy path so far avoided by the industrial nations.

The vision outlined in this article may be bold given current realities. Yet I am convinced that the twenty-first century is the era of renewable energies. I agree with Robert Jungk, the German futurologist, who said; "Bringing about the solar age is the fateful question for the future of mankind" (*Der Spiegel* 161.) ❖

References

Department of Energy, *National Energy Strategy*, February 1991. *Der Spiegel*, 34, 1987.

Flavin, Christopher, and Nicholas Lenssen. *Beyond the Petroleum Age*. Worldwatch Paper 100, December 1990.

Flavin, Christopher. *State of the World*. Worldwatch Institute, 1990.

Gadgil, Ashok et al. *Conservation Potential of Compact Fluorescent Lamps in India and Brazil*. Lawrence Berkeley Laboratory, 1989.

Goldemberg, José et al. *Energy for a Sustainable World*. World Resources Institute, 1987.

National Academy of Sciences. *Policy Implications of Greenhouse Warming*, National Academy Press, 1991.

World Resources 1990-1991. Report by the World Resources Institute, UNEP and UNDP. Oxford UP, 1991.

World Resources 1992-1993. Report by the World Resources Institute, UNEP and UNDP, Oxford UP, 1992.

VIEWS FROM

_____

ECONOMICS

THE AGE OF EXTERNALITIES

– CARL PHILLIPS

True mastery can be gained by letting things go their own way. It can't be gained by interfering.

– Lao Tze, *Tao Te Ching*

If externalities are present, [then] profit-maximizing behavior will not necessarily lead to an efficient allocation of resources. How can we correct for this deficiency of the market mechanism?

– Hal Varian, *Microeconomic Analysis*

The cyclical nature of political and economic trends is a favorite topic of scholars and pundits. These discussions, however, tend to ignore the strictly monotonic trends that are primary driving forces in the future public policy environment. The most important of these trends is increasing population. Also important are the expanding sovereignty of individuals over their lives, increasing local diversity, and the increasing complexity of people's interactions. It is hardly bold to state that the specific implications of these four trends for public policy in the year 2000 and beyond are overwhelming. Indeed, identifying the resulting implications for various *specific* public policies over the next decade is such a common pastime that it almost seems redundant to make a list.

Perhaps more important than any of these specific effects is an implication for public policy making in general. Only by recognizing this broader trend can we predict the oncoming shift in the role of government in our lives. These four monotonic trends will

Carl Phillips is a doctoral candidate in public policy, focusing on an economic approach to public-private communications processes. His research emphasizes environmental economics and health policy. He holds a B.A. in math and history from The Ohio State University where he was graduated summa cum laude, *as well as a Master's degree in Public Policy from Harvard. Before entering the graduate program at Harvard, he worked for three years as an economic consultant.*

combine to increase the importance of the spillover effects or "externalities" of individual actions. The trends will tend to increase the frequency and magnitude of externalities, while reducing the opportunity for overcoming the problems they create through means other than government intervention. The result will be the need for governments (at all levels and throughout much of the world) to make dramatic shifts their emphasis and to increase their attention to these externalities.

ROLE OF GOVERNMENT

Governments exist for many reasons, some positive. They permit voluntary exchange by protecting property rights, facilitate the expansion of nations, protect the weak, and aggrandize the strong. Within the possible duties that would appear on people's lists of the proper roles of government, we would expect there to be some nontrivial, near universal intersection. What roles of government would show up on the list of any individual who thinks seriously about the question? Various commentators will reject, for example, the government's role in accumulating or using military power, even to defend one's own borders, or in redistributing wealth, even if there is great inequality. Ultimately, we might expect that this intersection will consist of policies that favor everyone, what economists call a Pareto improvement, a change that is no worse for anyone and strictly better for at least one person. It is hard to envision a reasonable philosophy of the role of government that would not support policies that achieve such improvements.

Achieving Pareto improvements might at first seem like a trivial duty for government. But it turns out that there are compelling reasons to believe that as the governed state becomes more populous and the world becomes more complicated, such matters evolve from a fairly subtle role for government to the primary role of government.

EXTERNALITIES AND COASE

Why are there Pareto improvements available that the market cannot achieve on its own? After all, achieving all possible "gains from trade" is supposed to be the purpose (or at least the forte) of free markets. The problem stems from the market failure known as externalities. An externality arises when one person's action affects the utility or level of well being of another person who is uninvolved with the decision to take the action. Classic examples of externalities include the effects of polluting the air (causing the polluter's neighbors to suffer), crowding of the streets by driving at rush hour (each driver delaying the others), and furthering one's education (increasing the benefits one brings to society).

The first two of these have negative effects on others' well being (negative externalities), whereas the last tends to have a positive spillover to others (positive externality).

Even with the existence of externalities, the question remains: why does the market fail to achieve these results on its own? Indeed, the celebrated Coase Theorem, named after the 1991 Nobel laureate in economics, states that given certain conditions, the market will take care of all externalities—those who are suffering from (or gaining from) externalities will cut a deal with whoever is causing the externalities to get to a Pareto optimal outcome (Coase 1-44). The conditions that allow this ideal outcome are critical, however, and the monotonic trends stated above move us further from fulfilling them.

If Coasian bargains are to achieve an optimal outcome, property rights for everything must be well established and the cost of transactions—that is, the cost of bargaining and carrying out the promises made—must be zero. For example, consider the case of two neighbors, one who wants to have a loud party and the other who has the right to peace and quiet. Since we have declared a property right for peace and quiet, the potential partier must "purchase" the opportunity to interfere with that right, presumably by doing something for or giving something to the quiet neighbor. The bargain is nearly costless (two neighbors talking), and the property right being traded is well established (there is a right to quiet).

Now, consider an example where a firm wants to pollute the air, but the local residents will suffer more from the pollution than the firm will gain. If clean air were a well defined right of the residents, they would refuse to sell it and avoid the pollution that is "inefficient" in that it has a high net cost. Even if the firm had the right to pollute, if it were costless for everyone to bargain, the residents could get together and pay the firm to not pollute. However, without government intervention there is no well established property right for clean air, which implicitly leaves the factory with the right to pollute. We would like the people to get together and convince the firm not to pollute, but the transaction costs, which stem from the sheer difficulty of getting everyone together and what are known as "free rider" or collective actions problems, make this unlikely.

It is in cases like this that the externalities and the lack of market mechanisms to solve them warrant government intervention. That intervention can consist of limiting the allowable quantity of pollution, taxing pollution, cleaning up the pollution, or any of a number of other policies. Without going into the details of possible interventions, we can imagine that the government will figure out the "right" level of pollution—in this case either none or a limited amount—and impose a policy that achieves this level, reducing the externality. With such interventions we may find ourselves leaving the realm of true Pareto improvements and entering the wider realm of potential Pareto improvements. That is, we have achieved the outcome that the Coasian bargain would achieve, except for making the actual payment rendering the outcome a true Pareto improvement. In this case, the polluter may be required to reduce pollution without actually collecting the reward that market would have offered. In its attempt to make a true Pareto improvement, the government could devise a way to transfer wealth from those who win to those who lose.

Thus, it becomes clear that laws and regulations dealing with pollution, zoning, preserving natural resources, and prohibiting general nuisances are all largely concerned with minimizing the negative externalities that people might impose on each other if they were allowed to do what they wanted. In terms of a vision for the future, why does this represent a fundamental trend in the nature of governments' duties? It turns out that the four monotonic trends described at the outset will tend to combine to increase the number of externalities and move the world further from the Coasian conditions for market solutions.

POPULATION GROWTH

The primary driving force behind the increase in externalities is population growth. The potential for externalities increases roughly proportionally to the square of the population. (Strictly speaking, it increases with the square of the population density, but most governments preside over a fixed land area, so this does not differ by much. The distinction becomes more significant to the extent that there is increasing urbanization, which causes the population density to increase faster than the population.) To see why this is the case, consider a town of fixed size where on any given day each person "encounters" each other person exactly once. An encounter between individual X and Y is any opportunity for X to impose an externality on Y, such as X's factory polluting the air that Y breathes, X playing Frisbee on a sidewalk where Y is trying to walk, or X and Y being in the same traffic jam, in which case we might have a two-way "encounter." If there are 100 people in the town, each will encounter each of the others, for a total of 9900 encounters, or just under 100 squared. With 200 people, there will be 39,800 encounters, just under 200 squared, and so on.

Even if we change from a deterministic "one encounter per person" world to a world with some random distribution of the number of encounters between any two people, the expected number of potential externalities still increases with the square of the population. Looked at another way, if we double the population, then we double the number of factories that are producing pollution and double the number of people who are suffering from the pollution, increasing the magnitude of the externalities by a factor of four.

With a small population, there is no crowding, pollution is fairly minor, and natural resources are only minimally depleted. The total magnitude of externalities is minor enough that it is more costly for the government to interfere than for it to just allow them to continue. As the population grows, we need zoning boards, toll roads, and an Environmental Protection Agency. As the population continues to grow, previously tolerated nuisances become too costly to endure. Los Angeles is phasing in requirements for pollution-free cars because the externalities from auto exhaust have become intolerable. Singapore, the most densely populated country in the world, has only one park where playing Frisbee is legal and imposes heavy fines for such externality-producing behavior as spitting on the sidewalk. As the population increases, the pleasure available from being able to play Frisbee wherever one wishes is exceeded in magnitude by the aggregate externality costs to those who wish to walk without being beaned by plastic.

INDIVIDUAL SOVEREIGNTY

Multiplying the effect of the increase in the number of encounters between individuals is the number of such encounters perceived as creating externalities. Government can be seen as creator and guarantor of individual liberty, a role in which it has made remarkable progress over the last few centuries in much of the world. Therein lies much of the problem of externalities. At the simplest level, this is caused by people having "freedom to." The more people are have freedom to act, the more actors there will be doing things that are costly to others. But, in many countries, including the United States, the level of individual freedom has already reached the point where most people are free to control most of their own actions. In the future, individual sovereignty will be the source of greater externalities in the future primarily due to "freedom from."

In the industrializing era, there was little sense of individuals having freedom from externalities. From a modern point of view, we find horrifying the costs imposed on innocent people, but from the perspective of the day, if these costs were not considered part of the social welfare, then there was no externality that needed to be corrected. Wealthier, better educated people demand more sovereignty over more aspects of their life. Today, people are much less willing to accept environmental toxins, to wait in long queues, or to risk accidents than they were a century, or even a few decades, ago. In the future, we can expect more and more demands by individuals that they not be subject to the spillovers from the actions of others. The result is more perceived externalities that must somehow be addressed.

From the Coasian point of view, this trend suggests that the property rights picture is becoming more complicated. If an externality— for example, possible harm from nearby high voltage power lines—is not recognized, then there is no known reason to intervene in the market. If the hazard is recognized but thought to be very minor, and no property rights to be protected from it exist, then nothing will change. The power company will continue to "pollute," and this will be efficient due to the perceived minor cost. The lack of a Coasian bargaining situation will not hurt because the default outcome, allowing the externality to continue, will be efficient.

But consider what happens as individual sovereignty increases and individuals establish the right to be free from power lines. Assuming that the externality damage is still minor, the social optimum is still to allow the power line. But, if we resort to a simple public policy solution, letting people protect their property rights by banning the power line, we will get a highly inefficient solution. The power company could theoretically pay off all those suffering from the power lines in a Coasian bargain, but the cost of identifying and bargaining with the effected individuals may be prohibitively high.

More generally, the very costly trend of NIMBY ("not in my back yard") politics can be traced to an increasing sense of the right to be free from the externalities caused by landfills, industrial sites, roadways, and countless other unwanted neighbors. In many such cases, the actual cost that might result from the "new" externalities is not the direct spillovers, but the complete prohibition of the activity that is causing them. Such prohibition is often much more costly than the externalities would have been. The result is a need for not only more frequent government intervention, but more sophisticated intervention to optimally address such situations.

LOCAL DIVERSITY

Further increasing the probability that any given encounter will produce an externality is the greater probability that the individuals involved will have very different values or norms of behavior. People from different cultures, religions, and socio-economic backgrounds live and work in close proximity to each other. This local diversity, brought about by the ease of travel and lowered barriers, raises the chance that one person will consider an action normal behavior, while his neighbor will find it highly deleterious.

In a relatively homogeneous population, the local norms for individual behavior that causes externalities, such as dumping trash beside the road, chopping down trees, playing loud music, or letting your pets run free, will be largely adhered to by everyone. Such norms will presumably achieve a roughly optimal outcome based on the values of that community. On a larger scale, appreciation of environmental protection, demands for traffic safety, and methods of personal courtesy will tend to be similar within groups of similar people. But as individuals with different convictions become neighbors, those who are accepting of any particular negative externality may engage in actions that are very costly to some of those around them. Major sources of externalities are behaviors that offend someone's religious beliefs. While it may not be appropriate or even possible for government to step in and eliminate such conflicts, it is uniquely positioned to try to minimize such conflicts and reduce the losses that are resulting from them.

As the number of externality-producing actions increases, the community standards that serve to reduce them may become confused and break down. In a more uniform population, the local authority figures would be available as arbiters of any conflict over externalities. With the reduction in influence of such institutions, the demand for government intervention grows louder.

INCREASING COMPLEXITY

While population increases drive up the number of encounters at a high rate and while sovereignty and diversity increase the probability that any encounter will lead to externalities, another trend is making it less likely that market mechanisms will be able to eliminate the externalities. The complexity of our society is increasing the cost of Coasian bargaining. As population increases, many externality situations are complicated by the number of parties who must be included in any Coasian bargain, thereby raising its costs. Another complicating factor is the inability to identify the source of, or sometimes even the existence of, an externality.

In a simpler world, if residents did not like local industrial pollution, they were likely to know where the externalities were coming from—the smoke and noise from the town blacksmith—and how to bargain for their reduction. While pursuing a Coasian bargain would still not be costless, it would be relatively inexpensive. This is not the case when the pollution in question is, for example, heavy metals leaking into a lake from somewhere, ruining recreational values, and the suspects are large firms with factories near the lake. The transaction cost of bargaining away this problem is high, but we could at least envision how a citizen group could organize and try to negotiate a better outcome. It becomes even harder to identify the source of the problem when the externality in question is radioactive leakage or radio wave interference with people's cellular phones.

Moreover, it is impossible to bargain with passing commuters, unreachable corporate executives of multinational conglomerates, or inanimate objects whose ultimate owner or controller is unknown. Modern scientific and engineering technology creates new sources of externality that most of us do not understand. Modern societal patterns separate causes from effects to such an extent that it is hard for individual citizens to determine who is to blame if they suffer. It would be ridiculously optimistic to think that government can pierce all the veils that are obscuring the sources of externalities and achieve the social optimum by fiat. But, as the collective agent for the population, government has a huge comparative advantage in trying to improving upon such situations as the cost of Coasian bargaining increases.

The inclination of the government to intervene in the free market and people's lives has some cyclical tendencies. But the demand for intervention to solve the problems surrounding negative externalities is growing monotonically and rapidly. More encounters between people and the greater probability that someone will view that encounter as creating an externality increase the magnitude of the benefits that can be gained by reducing the externalities. The increasing complexity of externality-producing situations leaves the government in a unique position to improve them. If governments fail to rise to these new challenges, the magnitude of the losses to everyone will be huge and will keep growing.

Even when government does rise to the occasion, however, we may not be completely pleased by the result. Ultimately, we have to realize that the governing of externalities will reverse the trend of government guaranteeing ever-expanding rights of the individual. The monotonic trends described here will have many troubling direct outcomes: sheer crowding, damage to the environment, marginalization of old skills and talents, growing anxiety, and more frequent confrontation. Beyond these, we might find particularly troubling the necessary and inevitable surrender of individual freedoms that come with the loss of elbow room. ❖

References

Coase, Ronald. "The Problem of Social Cost." *Journal of Law and Economics* 3 (1960: 1–44.

Lao-Tze, *Tao Te Ching.* Trans. Stephen Mitchell. New York: Harper and Row, 1988.

Varian, Hal. *Microeconomic Analysis.* New York: W. W. Norton & Company, 1984.

EVOLUTION TOWARD HUMANISTIC ECONOMIC SYSTEMS

– SHANTI RABINDRAN

E conomics in the year 2000 and beyond will be concerned with equity, ecology, and non-alienating work. Equity concerns will arise from the recognition of individuals' rights to basic needs of food, clothing, shelter, health, education, and non-alienating work, thereby making work itself more satisfying. Social institutions will be concerned with the well being of society, instead of merely perpetuating the self-interests of some individuals.

The critique of the premises of American capitalism will lead to reforms in global economic thought. Currently American capitalism is being exported to Eastern Europe and the Southern Hemisphere as *the* economic system that yields social prosperity. This wholesale export has come about because the demise of communism in the former Soviet Union and Eastern bloc states has been misinterpreted as the victory of American capitalism over communism. A closer examination of capitalism as practiced in the United States and of communism as practiced in the Soviet Union suggests that both systems share characteristics that do not satisfy the needs of the masses; hence, both systems risk being overthrown unless they are reformed.

In the former Eastern blocs states, production has been geared toward capital intensive machinery and weapon systems instead of basic consumer goods. An elite within the society, without input from the general public, defined goods that the society should produce. Similarly, many in the United States have lobbied for

Shanti Rabindran *is a junior on a Harvard/Radcliffe scholarship with a joint concentration in economics and in environmental science and public policy. She enjoys prodding conventional wisdom on economic "development." She acknowledges the influence of Stephen Marglin on the essay she has prepared for this volume.*

government expenditure on the military in lieu of worker training, public health, education, and social programs that would
assist others less fortunate to realize their potential. These systems
of production exist only as long as public opinion can be controlled. Public opposition in the former Eastern bloc states has
been oppressed by the threats of the state police and the Soviet
Red Army, whereas public opposition in the United States has
been tempered with more subtle manipulation of false promises
and premises. These premises include that the pursuit of self-
interest should be encouraged because it inevitably leads to the
improvement of the social welfare; that is, the affluence of the
wealthy business class would "trickle down" to the poor.

TOWARD ECONOMIC CHANGES

Fortunately, not everyone can be fooled all the time. As the
Eastern bloc citizens overthrew their former systems, the public,
policy makers, and economists in the United States and in other
countries influenced by American-styled capitalism are questioning the premises of this economic system. More attention is being
paid to the need to temper self-interest, to reorganize toward
production structures that do not alienate workers, to assist the
poor directly through state programs, and to recognize the ecological limits to production.

Among the fundamental premises in economic ideology being
questioned is the pursuit of self-interest. First, the environmental
and social degradation demonstrates the fallacy in the argument
that the pursuit of self-interest inevitably leads to the improvement
of the social welfare. In fact, private interests and social interests
often diverge, as the problem of environmental pollution shows.
Second, those who respond to stimuli from social institutions, may
not necessarily act in the narrow pursuit of self-interests if alternative values are accepted and induced by those institutions. Principles like a corporation's responsibility to workers' welfare should
nurture more cooperative attitudes and emphasize the social
good.

Economists and others often quote Adam Smith, the father of
economics, in arguing the virtues of promoting the individual's
self-interest. In pursuing their self-interests, individuals are assumed to contribute to the improvement of social welfare, as
Adam Smith envisioned:

> [The rich] consume little more than the poor; and in spite
> of their natural selfishness and rapacity; though they mean
> only their own convenience, though the sole end which
> they propose from the labors of all the thousands which

they employ be the gratification of their own vain and insatiable desires, they divide with the poor the produce of all their improvements. They are led by the invisible hand to make the same distribution of the necessaries of life which would have been made had the earth been divided into equal portions among its inhabitants; and thus without intending it, without knowing it, advance the interest of the society. (Cited in Lutz and Lux 28)

However, widespread pollution, which undermines the health and productive capacity of current and future generations, proves that private interests often diverge from the social good. The entrepreneur who merely pursues her self-interest incorporates the costs which she faces and ignores the costs borne by society. On economic self-interests alone, it is rational for her to increase production beyond a social optimum because all the benefits accrue to her while the costs are spread among members of society. In fact, passages from Smith's writings, which advocates of self-interest often overlook, warn of the need to temper self-interest in order to maintain a flourishing and happy society. For example, Smith writes:

All members of human society stand in need of each other's assistance and are likewise exposed to mutual injuries. When the necessary assistance is reciprocally afforded from love, from gratitude, and esteem, the society flourishes and is happy. All the different members of it . . . are drawn to one common center of mutual good offices. . . . Society, however, cannot subsist among those who are at all times ready to hurt and injure one another. The moment the injury begins, the moment that mutual resentment and animosity takes place, all the bands of it are broken asunder, and the different members of which it consisted are, as it were, dissipated and scattered abroad by violence and opposition of their discordant affections. (Cited in Lutz and Lux 28)

Human beings act in response to the environment and social institutions. In the United States, the pursuit of self-interest may not be a surprising outcome because this behavior was institutionally encouraged in the Reagan and Bush pro-business era. Under different social norms and institutions, different motivations for behavior may be induced. Hobson, the late London economist, writes:

Alterations in the organization and government of businesses and industries so as to give security of employment and of livelihood to workers, and some increased "voice" to them in the conditions of work, it seems reasonably possible to modify the conscious stress of personal gain-seeking and to educate a clearer sense of social solidarity and service. . . . Security is, therefore, the first essential in any shift of the relative appeal to personal and social motives. The second essential is such alterations in the government of businesses as to give the ordinary worker some real sense of participation in the conduct and efficiency of business. (Cited in Lutz and Lux 53)

NON-ALIENATING WORK

Hobson's argument finds support in the Japanese system. Although the Japanese system has been criticized for its bias against women in the workforce, the intense competition in schools, and its harm to the environment, Japanese workers have security of employment and a sense of participation in their firms. Japanese workers have a stronger sense of social solidarity and are less apt to overemphasize personal gain. Japanese firms are regarded by the community as responsible for the workers' well being, including the provision of lifetime employment. In return, workers pledge their loyalty and jointly work toward the success of their firm. In the American structure of production, workers are assumed to obtain their sense of fulfillment from goods on which they spend their wages. People work in assembly lines, with minimal creativity and are mere appendages in a large production structure in which they have no influence. Widespread dissatisfaction suggests that workers are unwilling to accept alienating work in exchange for the promises of wages at the day's end. Human beings do not derive their sense of well being merely from the consumption of material goods. We need meaningful work that challenges our creativity, provides opportunities for participation in the production process, and gives us a sense of self worth.

The right to livelihood is less recognized in the United States than in many other countries. In order to maintain profit levels, firms hire and fire workers at will. Unemployment is dismissed as an inevitable consequences of a dynamic economic system. Such attitudes do not encourage worker loyalty. With rampant job-hopping, firms cannot fully reap benefits from worker training. Therefore, American firms are less competitive as they invest less in worker training. Managers in American corporations are forced to pay more attention to making work in itself meaningful and encouraging worker participation.

Although many economists have focused more on the need for efficiency than on the problems of distribution of wealth, society is forced to deal with these problems for ethical reasons. Rawls argues that under the veil of ignorance, some individuals would choose redistributions that make the poorest members of society as wealthy as possible. The "haves" themselves may not tolerate disparities. Many Americans who have access to health care and who enjoy incomes beyond the poverty level do not accept that five million children are living in poverty in a country with one of the highest per capita GNPs, while five million others are without primary health care in a country that spends fourteen percent of its GNP on healthcare. The rich are not insulated from societal problems arising from the coexistence of dire poverty and affluence. Unemployment and the coexistence of poverty and affluence have led to high crime rates. The higher rates of violent crimes in the United States compared to those in Western Europe are correlated to the higher income disparities in this country. Some Europeans argue that their welfare programs—including universal access to health care, insurance, and retraining programs for the unemployed—help keep their crime rates lower than those in the United States. The poor may resort to violent revolution out of desperation and in part because they have nothing to lose in attempting to topple the status quo. The Shah of Iran, who paid insufficient attention to the poor masses and co-opted a rich elite, was violently overthrown by Muslim fundamentalists.

Many notions in economic thinking such as the so-called trickle-down effect, general prosperity arising from national income growth, and the freedom to move up the income ladder with hard work have been shown to be unrealistic. Many economists no longer accept the notion that a general increase in the average per capita income necessarily correlates to the improvement in the economic well being of a large percentage of the community. A writer in the *New York Times* of 5 May 1992 remarks:

> While the total income for all 66 million American families expanded by about $740 billion in inflation-adjusted dollars during the Carter-Reagan years, the slice belonging to the top 1 percent grew to 13% of all family income, up from 9%. The average pretax income of families in the top percent swelled to $560,000 from $315,000, for a 77% gain in a dozen years, again in constant dollars. At the same time the typical American family—smack in the middle, or at the median, of the income distribution—saw its income edge up only 4% to $36,000. At the bottom 40% of families had actual declines in income.

We now recognize that during the 1980s the rich got very richer and that the problems of inequality in the distribution of wealth continue to haunt society. The urgency to deal with this inequity between the rich and poor will continue to be felt in the next decade as well. In the *New York Times* (18 May 1992), Professor Danzinger, an economist at the University of Michigan, draws attention to this situation:

It became harder to climb out of poverty largely because of the . . . outright decline of real earnings among young, less-educated men. . . . The proportion of high school graduates likely to earn more than a poverty level income—which was $11,662 in 1989 dollars—fell to 88% in the 1980s from 93% in the 1970s among white men and to 75% from 84% among black men.

The widespread belief that American capitalism allows the realization of the American Dream, whereby one could reach the top with hard work and grit despite humble beginnings, is clearly fallacious. As Professor Katz of Harvard has argued, "the best predictor for how well you'll do is still how well your parents did. . . . It is not a lottery in which people with high school degrees or poor parents have just as much chance of getting to the top as someone with college degrees and rich parents. People with less education are systematically falling behind" (cited in the *New York Times,* 18 May 1992).

ECOLOGY

Because the environment cannot continue to assimilate pollution at current levels and because technological "quick fixes" have not been successful in overcoming the earth's limitations, ecology will remain an important issue in the next decades. The tremendous increase in dump sites and cases of contamination of ground water, soil, as well as of habitats that are said now to be biologically dead, sends a clear signal that human activities are approaching the limits of the earth's carrying capacity. The Green Revolution, which had been hailed the human conquest of our earth's limit is extremely problematic. High-yield varieties of some plants demand more use of biocides and water, and they are susceptible to environmental vagaries. Pesticides have led to the evolution of more resistant strains, contaminated ground water, health problems, and deaths. Recent technological fixes proposed to curb environmental problems such as fertilizing the oceans to increase oceanic uptake of carbon dioxide illustrate the impossibility of engineering outcomes in a complex system we know little about.

In attempting to fix the greenhouse warming problem, we risk disrupting the food chain by artificially stimulating the growth of a different species composition.

Economics in the next decade will be concerned about all of these issues. Self interest, as the motivating force behind economic relationships, is unlikely to be gradually abandoned in favor of a reorganization of production structures that do not alienate workers. We will, however, see more attempts to assist the poor through state programs and to recognize the ecological limits to production. Economists and policy makers will be forced to respond to this increasing demand for more humanistic economic systems, emphasizing the individual's rights to basic needs and a high quality of life, while at the same time incorporating responsible ecological considerations. As we enter the next millennium, more global ethical considerations beyond those of narrow self-interest will be essential. As it is callously inhumane to demand sacrifice from those who are struggling to fulfill their basic needs, society needs to encourage the affluent to examine their conspicuous consumption. As Adam Smith declared, "Man . . . ought to regard himself, not as something separated and detached, but as a citizen of the world, a member of the vast commonwealth of nature . . . . To the interest of this great community, he ought at all times [to acknowledge] that his own little interest should be sacrificed" (*Theory of Moral Sentiments,* quoted in Sen 23). ❖

References

Lutz, Mark, and Kenneth Lux. *The Challenge of Humanistic Economics.* Menlo Park: Benjamin/Cummings Publishing Company, 1979.

New York Times. 5 March and 18 May 1992.

Sen, Amartya. *Ethics and Economics.* Cambridge: Basil Blackwell, 1987.

VIEWS FROM

BUSINESS

BUSINESS BEYOND BORDERS

– ANDREW F. POPELL

B y the year 2000 a large part of the business world will be
much closer to being "borderless." The traditional definition of a company will change as the typical boundaries between company and suppliers, employees and customers
are breached. At the global level the concept of national borders
will fade with regard to the trade of goods and services, the free
flow of information, immigration, and the idea of national corporations. Prompted by changes in demographics, lifestyles, and new
demands from customers, the physical borders of the office will be
transcended by new information technology. Not only will the
world in which we work be different, but we ourselves will be
different. As the traditional psychic and physical borders that tie
us to our country, company, and office dissolve, individual freedom and identity will rise. Already, in practice, much of the world
lives in a borderless state. Kenichi Ohmae, Managing Director of
McKinsey & Company in Japan, has referred to the roughly one
billion people living in the economic triad of Japan, the European
Economic Community, and the United States (and satellite advanced economies such as Hong Kong, Taiwan, and Singapore) as
an Interlinked Economy (ILE). By this he means that in this part
of the world there will be a free flow of goods, services, technology,
people, and corporations (xi, xiii).

Ohmae believes that many of the Eastern European nations and
some of the emerging industrialized nations in Asia will join the
ILE. As the educational level of its people increases and it develops
an information infrastructure, Mexico should also soon join this
group of nations. South American nations such as Chile and
Venezuela will followed later.

The current conflicts between France and the EEC over agricul-

---

*Andrew F. Popell was born in Buenos Aires, Argentina, and grew up in Woodside,
California. He received an A.B. in Government with a concentration in interna-
tional relations from Harvard in 1987 and will complete his studies at the
Harvard Business School in 1993. He has worked as marketing manager at Oracle
Corporation, a database software company, and in September he plans to start
Passion for Learning, a mail order company for children's educational products.*

tural subsidies, as well as between Japan and the United States over trade barriers, are evidence that we have not yet reached a pure Interlinked Economy, but we are making rapid progress on many fronts. Already most countries in the ILE have access to goods and services with minimal restrictions. Through agreements such as GATT and NAFTA, trade in the future will move closer to being more free than it is today. While it seems as if we are moving in fits and starts toward unrestricted trade, the global consumer will make reaching the ILE an inevitability. Contemplating this point, I began to think of where my various possessions came from and realized that I owned a couple of Italian suits, a pair of French skis, a Japanese car, and an American computer. Like the customers Ohmae describes as having a power generated by a lack of national allegiance, I am much more interested in the quality and price of a product than who made it.

Customer allegiance to quality rather than origin is further intensified by advances in information technology. With technology like satellite dishes and global electronic mail networks, people around the world can see how everyone else is living and what toys they are playing with. This technology helps spread national cultures and political ideology around the world. National borders are also disappearing because of the flow of information, technology, and expertise. Increasingly, companies will design products in one country, gather the best available technology from various other countries, and assemble these products in yet other countries. Japanese computer companies, for example, will design computers in Japan, buy some components like Intel chips from the United States, and manufacture the machines in Korea.

The movement of people will also be much freer in the future. Already, through agreements like NAFTA and the EEC there is, at the continental level, increasing free immigration. While there is a danger that the globe will be spilt into trading blocks in the short run, as income disparities decrease and economies become more intertwined, these barriers should also disappear.

In order to prevent the adverse effects of currency fluctuations and protectionism and get closer to local customers, corporations themselves will move freely from country to country, resulting in the blurring of the concept of the national company. Indicative of this trend, Reebok and Toyota are becoming borderless companies. Originally a British company, Reebok is now American owned and manufactures its shoes in Korea. Toyota builds some of its cars on U.S. soil, with fifty percent American parts and American labor. According to an article in *Business Week* (12 April 1993), Toyota plans to buy $2 billion of the $3.8 billion in parts that its

U.S. plants will need in 1994 from traditional U.S. suppliers. Under such an organization, the concept of a Japanese car becomes meaningless.

The traditional way of defining corporations will change as the borders between companies and their suppliers, employees, and customers begin to disappear. More corporations will integrate operations with their suppliers as traditional methods of ordering and delivery can no longer meet customer demands. In order to become more efficient, companies will have to increase their quality, decrease their costs, and turn out products faster. They will have no choice other than to integrate with their suppliers if they want to compete against increasingly global competition.

Calyx & Corolla, a seller of fresh flowers by mail, epitomizes the company moving toward this integration. Ruth Owades, the company's founder, describes her philosophy: "I envisioned a table with three legs and Calyx & Corolla was only one of them. The other was the best flower growers available, and the third was Federal Express, the number one air carrier" (6). At least twice a day, Calyx & Corolla transmits orders by modem to its select group of growers. There, a Calyx & Corolla account manager, employed by the grower, supervises the selection of the order and its preparation. The growers and Calyx & Corolla can track shipments on-line through the computer terminals placed at their offices by Federal Express.

The same competitive pressures that will make companies integrate with their suppliers will make them redefine the relationship between the company and its employees. Forced to reduce overhead costs and increase worker creativity and motivation, companies will trade traditional job-specific hierarchies for teams of employees able to perform multiple functions. Corporations will also reduce the number of employees by seeking sources outside the company to do the work previously done in-house. For example, Oracle Corporation, a large database software company, already has creative account managers who coordinate and monitor teams of freelance designers, writers, and photographers who produce marketing materials for internal clients. This system reduces Oracle's overhead costs, increases the freelancers' motivation, and reduces the probability that internal groups produce unnecessary marketing materials.

Again, with the new focus on the customer and competitive pressure, companies will have to find innovative ways to meet customer needs. Already, companies are finding ways to successfully integrate customers into their operations. Discovery Toys eschews the traditional retail method and uses customers to promote and sell their products. Automotive companies are moving towards enabling customers to go to a dealership, choose among dozens of options, and receive their customized vehicle within a few weeks. With advances in automation and manufacturing, more and more corporations will integrate and involve their clients in order to customize products and services to meet the new demands of a global market.

Not only will business relationships be borderless, but the space in which they take place will also be without physical boundaries. Employees of the corporation of the past have worked in large central headquarters or at large regional sales office or manufacturing facilities. A growing number of these people will work in smaller and smaller regional offices, at home, or in completely nontraditional work spaces.

The need to increase integration with suppliers and customers will necessitate the move away from headquarters. This move will be facilitated by new information technology such as teleconferencing, electronic mail, and faxes, as well as by advances in transportation such as floating bullet trains. Such improvements in telecommunications and transportation will give people the opportunity to work out of their homes, increasing their flexibility to go to the corporate office at more convenient times and making them much more productive. Because of the greater demand for affordable child care and the worsening congestion and traffic in big cities, there will be a surge in the amount of time that people will opt to work at home.

The move toward borderless relationships and borderless offices will create an impetus to redefine the traditional work space. Car faxes, airplane phones, laptop computers, and cellular technology are all elements of the emerging mobile office; employees will be able to work anywhere in the world, under more productive conditions, and closer to company suppliers and customers. Frito-Lay exemplifies the use of one type of mobile office. All delivery people have computers in their trucks from which they can track stock levels at each store, information that can be combined with data from headquarters in order to give each store suggestions on how to improve the performance of underproducing brands.

The reality of business beyond borders will have a profound and revolutionary impact on individuals, corporations, and countries. On the individual level there will be a blending of work time and leisure time as traditional time borders—the 9-to-5 workday and 40-hour workweek— are eliminated in favor of flexible, task based work. The effect on individuals will be an increase in individual identity and personal liberty for those possessing the necessary skills and living within the Integrated Economy. These are the commonly cited "knowledge workers" of tomorrow.

Undereducated workers or those living in developing nations without the right information technology and transportation infrastructure will be left out until they are able to meet global competitive standards. Individuals, corporations, and governments moving beyond their own borders provide an example and means for these people eventually to find a niche in the borderless global society.

Companies that integrate with suppliers, employees, and customers will be able to become more efficient, cost-effective, and quality oriented, enabling them to meet their customers' needs and remain competitive. Large governmental institutions like the military and many parts of the bureaucracy will be much less needed. Therefore, national governments will have to redefine their roles as they become more and more integrated into the Interlinked Economy.

The Global Interlinked Economy is inevitable, but there are various factors that could slow this movement down. Nationalism is one of these forces. As we have seen with the EEC, the liberalized Eastern European nations, religious fundamentalism, jingoistic sentiments, and the fear of losing national culture and independence have been major stumbling blocks to achieving a borderless state. Analogous to nationalism, the "not-invented-here" syndrome prevents companies from recognizing the need to operate beyond corporate borders. On a more individual level, managers may be reluctant to relinquish personal control. This tendency toward empire building could prevent the flow of resources, employees, and ideas that is essential to a borderless corporation.

From personal risk aversion to corporate conservatism to protective national policies, one of the most pervasive and dangerous impediments to reaching a state of business beyond borders will be the fear of change. This borderless existence offers great potential for increased productivity and personal freedom. Given the opportunities for advancement, our biggest fear should be *not* changing. ❖

References

"Calyx & Corolla." Harvard Business School Case #9-592-035 (rev. 1992).

"Frito-Lay, Inc.: A Strategic Transition." Harvard Business School Case #9-187-065 (1991).

Ohmae, Kinichi. *The Borderless World.* New York: HarperBusiness, 1990.

PRESERVING THE COMMON GOOD:

THE ROLE OF FOR-PROFIT AND NOT-FOR-PROFIT ENTERPRISES
– IAN ROWE

Their value is normally demonstrated after tragedy—after a horrific famine causes wide-spread death and disease in a distant land, after a spectacular hurricane or tornado ravages countless lives and homes in its path of destruction, after saddening and pernicious riots wreak havoc upon the streets of urban America. While major organizations such as the Red Cross that perform in times of crisis are the most well-known, the not-for-profit sector plays a role in our society which has become almost indispensable. I hold a vision of a world becoming increasingly *more* reliant upon the services and products provided by not-for-profit organizations and a society no longer monopolized by the complementary public and private sectors.

Not-for-profits deliver outstanding teachers to devastated and underresourced public schools (Teach For America). They protect the rights of individuals across the globe (Amnesty International). They prevent environmental disaster, offer prenatal care to poor pregnant mothers, and provide housing for the homeless. Not-for-profits encompass museums, universities, healthcare providers, family planning clinics, and community centers. They provide a number of unglamorous services critical to communities that otherwise would be underserved by either the public or private sector. It is difficult today to imagine the fabric of our society *not* unraveling without the involvement of strong, proactive not-for-profit institutions, and this will be true even more so in the future.

Ian Rowe was born in London, England and reared in Jamaica, West Indies and New York City. He is a 1993 M.B.A. graduate of the Harvard Business School and was the first black Editor-in-Chief of the Harbus News, *the School's official newspaper. He will be the Executive Vice-President of Marketing for TEACH!, a new revenue-generating arm of Teach for America.*

FREE ENTERPRISE AS A CREATOR OF SOCIAL GOOD

In theory, the delicate relationship between the public sector and private enterprise is the source for social and economic prosperity. The freedom of private businesses to operate competitively for profit with minimal government regulation is the basis of modern capitalism. Not surprisingly, virtually no traditional economic or social philosophy identifies a need for any assembly of organizations whose mission is *not* to generate economic surplus, but rather is to accomplish altruistic objectives. Economists even posit that social benefits would be *jeopardized* if business institutions deemed social benevolence their primary motivation. Adam Smith argues that a merchant

> neither intends to promote the public interest, nor knows how much he is promoting it. . . . He is in this, as in many other cases, led by an invisible hand to promote an end which was no part of his intention. Nor is it always the worse for society that it was no part of it. By pursuing his own interest he frequently promotes that of the society more effectually than when he really intends to promote it. I have never known much good done by those who affected to trade for the public good. (1.18)

The noted economist Milton Friedman contends that "there is one and only one social responsibility of business—to use its resources and engage in activities designed to increase its profits." Ultimately, an ardent pursuit of profit is the *catalyst* for improved social conditions. Therefore, the common good—equal opportunity, individual freedom and social justice—is not the objective but a pleasant by-product of a free market strategy based wholly upon profit maximization and not driven by any socially responsible agenda. These market theories assume perfect competition; that markets are free of unfair discrimination; that consumers have access to and have full understanding of complete information; that all resources are productively utilized; that both markets and governments are efficient. But these assumptions are simply not valid in practice.

NOT-FOR-PROFITS FILL THE VOID

Government is rife with bureaucracy and inefficiency, limiting its ability to cure social ills. Simultaneously, private industry has an economic *disincentive* to serve communities that lack financial strength or political influence, retarding its desire to provide opportunities for advancement. The public and private sectors cannot be the only engines that generate economic wealth and stimulate social progress. In a recent article in the *Wall Street Journal*, Peter Drucker estimated that today the unrecognized not-for-profit sector comprises over 900,000 institutions with close to 90 million Americans working on staff or as volunteers. The economist John Byrne notes that this sector garners $104 billion in contributions annually (66). This phenomenal growth indicates that free market arguments overlook a critical aspect of societal development—that some organizations *must* exist solely for benevolent purposes. Not-for-profits act as a safety net for individuals caught between the public sector's inability to fulfill completely the essential needs of society (such as education and healthcare) and the private sector's proclivity to serve only constituencies that have economic power.

This abyss created between the private and public sectors is probably the most critical challenge threatening this country's future. As our society becomes increasingly more fragmented—economically, culturally and geographically—and confidence in the effectiveness of government dwindles, the need will grow for both market and nonmarket solutions to fill the void. The economist Kenneth Arrow states that "when the market fails to achieve an optimal state, society will, to some extent at least, recognize the gap, and nonmarket social institutions will arise attempting to bridge it." Social cohesiveness will depend upon potent not-for-profit institutions working in concert with a business community more committed to incorporating social values into their decision-making processes. According to Drucker, "the demand for socially responsible organizations will not go away, but rather widen" ("New Society").

REDEFINING THE SOCIAL ROLE OF BUSINESS INSTITUTIONS

Proponents of free-market theory proclaim that the failure of socialist bureaucracies and the continuous decline of public institutions will result in increased opportunities for for-profit enterprise to capitalize upon. Professor Greg Dees of the Harvard Business School believes that "With . . . privatization and the expansion of business into government functions and other fields (such as healthcare and social services) formerly dominated by non-profit institutions, the significance of business and the power of business managers should continue to grow." But this power may be corrupted unless accompanied by a shift in attitude towards business's role in preserving the social contract.

Acting solely for the common good and solely to attain maximum earnings are theoretically mutually exclusive, with business's responsibility normally falling on the latter. In practice, however, social objectives overlap with business's economic objectives, primarily because *acting in the social interest has economic value!* The new paradigm is that being socially responsible pays. Companies like Ben & Jerry's, the Body Shop, and Stride Rite have realized significant economic gains by conducting business in a socially conscious manner. While business should not exist entirely for social purposes, addressing social concerns will clearly play a significant role in determining which actions are to be taken to maximize profits. Cases in point are the growing business opportunities enjoyed by companies now focused on environmental protection. Heightened demand for waste reduction services, environmentally sensitive technologies, and the rise of environmental consulting groups demonstrate the vast market created as a result of increased "green" awareness. Prior to events such as Earth Day and public outrage over numerous environmental mishaps, these business opportunities simply did not exist in the same degree.

Successful managers of the future must be encouraged to pursue objectives which create goodwill (and subsequently greater sales) for their organizations. Acting as agents to maximize shareholder return, managers would be absolutely delinquent if the *impact of being socially negligent were not incorporated into their decisions.* The potential negative impact of public outcry, employee revolt, or failure to keep up with innovative competitors demands that managers be cognizant of the social implications of their actions. It is not that business leaders should become responsible *for* society, but rather that they should be responsible *to* society. Their primary concern is not the well-being of society, but how the repercussions of their decisions on society affects the well-being of their organization.

Fundamentally, business institutions would be naïve to act in any interest other than their own. That is their mission and their charge. Increasingly, however, society will value those actions taken by business which improve the common good or, at least, do not contribute to its decline. Being wholly focused on creating economic wealth will not absolve business from acting for social betterment, because the latter will need to be given careful consideration in order to achieve the former.

Broadening the Impact of Not-For-Profit Enterprise

A greater penetration of private business in traditionally public functions is an inevitable result of government's shrinking ability to provide basic social services. However, the rate of for-profit business expansion in these areas will depend upon the speed at which society places economic value on the services provided by these potential businesses. Otherwise, economic inviability will always be a barrier to entry for for-profit enterprises. Services like combating family violence, treating dying AIDS patients, wiping out illiteracy, and reducing drug abuse offer little economic upside for would-be entrepreneurs. Not-for-profits, by contrast, are not restricted by these financial hurdles and will continue to keep pace with society's unmet needs.

Moreover, when compared to for-profit organizations, the not-for-profits are in an advantageous position to expand into their business activities. Capitalizing on expertise developed over years of providing free or low-cost services, many not-for-profits are now engaging in revenue-generating activities to further their organizational missions. Whereas for-profits must wait for a change in the social valuation of services to make a particular business opportunity economically appealing, not-for-profits can initiate entrepreneurial activities as this shift evolves. Moreover, not-for-profits have the added advantage of tax exemption and continued access to financial support from foundations and other grant-giving organizations to subsidize these activities. Therefore, not-for-profits will be quicker than traditional for-profit entrepreneurs to take advantage of income generating opportunities focused on the social arena. As Drucker forecasts, "The nonprofits have the potential to become America's social sector—equal in importance to the public sector of government and the private sector of business".

At the heart of our society is a vital network of not-for-profit organizations helping people. They exist because government is incapable of solving all of society's problems and because economic realities dampen the private sector's motivation to generate opportunities for wealth in indigent or otherwise unattractive communities. Simply put, not-for-profits succeed where the joint cooperation of the public and private sectors fails. It is the combination of these organizations pursuing higher purposes as well as the emerging development of more socially responsible businesses that makes my vision of the future so optimistic. Indeed, the trio of mutually supportive sectors—public, private, *and* social—will ultimately preserve the common good and enhance the public welfare of all citizens. ❖

References

Arrow, Kenneth. "Uncertainty and the Welfare Economics of Medical Care." *American Economic Review,* December 1963.

Byrne, John. "Profiting from the Nonprofits." *Business Week,* 26 March 1990, 66.

Dees, Greg. "Profits, Markets, and Values." Harvard Business School, January 1993.

Drucker, Peter. "It Profits Us to Strengthen Nonprofits." *Wall Street Journal,* December 1991.

———, "The New Society of Organizations." *Harvard Business Review,* September–October 1992.

Friedman, Milton. "The Social Responsibility of Business Is to Increase Its Profits." *New York Times Magazine,* 13 September 1970.

Smith, Adam. *An Inquiry into the Nature and Causes of the Wealth of Nations.* Ed. Edwin Cannan. Chicago: U of Chicago P, 1976.

A VIEW FROM

EDUCATION

EL SEÑOR BURBUJAS

– MARK TAYLOR

The secret of education lies in respecting the pupil.

– Emerson

No bubble is so iridescent or floats longer than that blown by the successful teacher.

– Sir William Osler

Mr. Moderno is preparing for a meeting with Mrs. Kiljoy for whom he has worked this semester during her maternity leave. He carefully places various drawings and essays in neat stacks on the large desk in the rear of the room as outside there are familiar sounds of children passing to their next class. The warning bell rings and the sounds become more excited as the last rush begins to avoid tardiness. He looks around the room. The walls are covered in butcher paper and are themselves covered in the scrawl of many different hands. The front board is clean with the exception of a colorful rendering of the word of the week "transcendence" and in large capital letters "EL SEÑOR BURBUJAS." He looks up at the clock. Mrs. Kiljoy is tardy.

There is a knock at the door. "Come in," calls Mr. Moderno. The door swings open and in strides Mrs. Kiljoy armed with a can of cleanser, rubber gloves, and a sponge. "Hello!" she smiles not quite falsely, "How are you?"

Mr. Moderno has risen and is crossing the room toward her. "I'm well, thank you. I am so glad you could make it." She passes

Mark Taylor *is a Master's candidate at the Harvard Graduate School of Education, having received his undergraduate degree in English literature from UCLA. His interests range from writing to sorcery, which he acknowledges some people may see as the same thing. This short story was first written as a response to a final exam question about human potential in Professor Vernon Howard's Philosophy of Education extension course. The epigraphs to this piece he located by accident or by sorcery while browsing in a Manhattan bookstore.*

him by and heads straight for the desk, looking around her at the room as she goes. She slides the neat piles over as she places her bucket and supplies in the center of the desk. The pile of drawings slips over the edge and scatters as it falls to the floor.

"Oops! Sorry!" says Mrs. Kiljoy, "Were those important?"

"To the artist." Mr. Moderno laughs as he kneels to pick them up.

Mrs. Kiljoy turns to open the file cabinet behind the desk which is locked and has remained locked all semester. Surprised, she turns to him and asks, "Do you have the key to the file cabinet? I want to put my purse away."

"I do not have that key," Mr. Moderno responds calmly. "You did not leave it for me."

"I am quite sure I left it on the key ring that I gave to the main office," she insists. Mr. Moderno produces the ring and hands it to her. She examines it after which she pulls out her own keys. Locating the key on her own ring, she looks at Mr. Moderno quite shocked and apologetic. "I'm sorry! I was sure I had left you this." She pauses. "Whatever did you do for supplies? All of the tests were in there, and the spelling lists, and the guide for free time."

Mr. Moderno now looks puzzled. "I had at least thirty students per class in five classes a day. That was all the supplies I needed. Shall we begin our meeting?" he asks. "We only have a few minutes before homeroom ends. I have saved all of the lesson plans that the class has followed since you left, and some interesting examples of the work produced."

She shakes her head and quite sure of her married and middle class self, says, "I know these kids already. I can only imagine what has transpired with this drawer locked all semester. What did you do for vocabulary words? You did do vocabulary words, didn't you?"

"Oh yes! Yes, of course!" he replies. "In fact, I have samples for you here on the desk. If you'll have a seat, I'd love to show you some."

She seats herself, and he hands her one of the piles that was not disrupted by the purification supplies. She looks at it briefly. "But there are only five words on this list! I always gave at least thirty words a week. This list won't keep them busy fifteen minutes." She looks at him for confirmation.

"Ah, yes," he begins. "Well, after looking at the quality of use of those words in the students' writing samples, we decided to shorten the list and broaden the understanding."

"We decided?" she asks.

"Yes. The class and myself." He offers her another pile.

"You didn't let them take the dictionaries home, did you?"

"No. In fact, we only had one person use the dictionary. The rest of us attempted to define the words first and consulted the dictionary only when we were satisfied that our definition was acceptable to the group."

"I cannot imagine that working well with this bunch of kids," says Mrs. Kiljoy. "Half of them don't speak English most of the time anyway."

"Precisely," says Mr. Moderno. "That is why we worked on it as a group. After all, language is the means through which we have access to the group, our own ideas, and the ideas of others."

"What about tests? How will they be prepared for the state qualifiers?" she asks.

"We had many tests." Mr. Moderno smiles and adds, "Many tests and essays and outside assignments. But the most productive time was spent in discussions." He hands her the list of discussion topics.

She reads them out loud, "'What is History?' 'The AIDS Virus: Fact from Fiction.' 'Empowerment: Word or Way of Living?'" She looks incredulous. "You don't expect me to believe that they actually discussed these issues?"

"I expect nothing of you. I only offer this information so that your efforts with these children will not have to duplicate any of my own," says Mr. Moderno. "Please understand, I am not saying this was an easy thing to produce either. At first, they tried, but failed. They had rudimentary writing skills, at best. Apparently essay exams in your class were—how shall I say it?—underutilized. So we began our work in the realm of ideas where all were equally capable of contributing although some, admittedly, with more imagination and relevance. Then we would break up into groups with one student as leader who could synthesize these ideas into complete sentences. When I felt we had progressed to the next level, we worked on paragraphs, and then essays. Finally we evolved to individual essay form. We kept the papers very short with the understanding that a longer paper would require more of the same type of work."

"But did you impress upon them the importance of dates? Of memorizing the information required on the state mandated exam?" Mrs. Kiljoy asks.

"Why, yes, of course," answers Mr. Moderno. "First we examined the test from last year. We determined its social relevance as a tool for measuring our retention of facts associated with idealized Western European historical perspectives. Then we broadened those ideas to include our own perception of our place in the spectrum of experience of the modern world. We learned about our connections to History when our study was broadened to encompass the experiences of all cultures. And then we moved on."

"On to what? Curing cancer?" asks Mrs. Kiljoy.

"I can appreciate your skeptical humor, Mrs. Kiljoy, but I think others might see it as sarcasm. When I took over for you last fall, you told me to do as I wished with the class and with a quick dusting of the chalk from your hands, you left. It did not take me long to realize that your classes were run with the sole intention of adhering to rules and disseminating information, both of which have a place in education. However, I believe you saw the gap between what skills these children lacked and the potential for scholastic exchange as insurmountable, and adjusted your methods accordingly. I saw that gap as the place in which true learning, joyous and unbridled, begins. That is to say, when the learner knows the rules, has access to information, and begins the journey that will last a lifetime as a thinking individual, capable of choosing, of understanding reason and emotion and the need for both. Free to participate in a larger vision of the world."

"All of this?" She gestures to the walls. "Free to write on walls? To draw meaningless cartoons?"

"Pictures and words," adds Mr. Moderno. "When an assignment is complete and all work turned in, an individual has the opportunity to express a thought or an idea. No profanity is allowed and nothing degrading to others is permitted, or the writer loses all privileges at the paper. No one broke these rules."

"I know better than to allow gang style writing in my classroom!" Mrs. Kiljoy announces as if she is addressing a class.

"Let's be honest, Mrs. Kiljoy. You allowed no writing in your classroom."

"You insult me, Mr. Moderno. I have rules and standards to which they must adhere."

"No doubt. And traditions and hierarchies and prejudices."

"But you can't encourage this ghetto mentality, or you limit their potential," she adds decisively.

"On the contrary, Mrs. Kiljoy. I don't encourage anything but the exploration of ideas and self definition of potential, ghetto or otherwise. No matter how much cleaning solution you use, you can never scrub away the color of their skin or the neighborhood in which they live. They have experienced the world until this point. They will continue to experience. My goal within the context of this History class has been to give them the means to cut through anyone's preconceptions about the limits of their own potential and, in so doing, to redefine themselves, to reexamine their understanding of the world in which they live and learn. If it were not for Scantron testing and mindless repetition, what would the children actually learn in your classroom besides the one lesson that many of them learn early: What you think matters less than what the teacher thinks?"

The bell rings announcing the end of this class period. Mr. Moderno takes his own bucket from beneath the desk already filled with some soapy water and a little glycerin. "Today we study that lesson in case you would like to watch." He continues talking to her as he walks to the front of the room. "Today we learn to blow bubbles. We examine the bubbles blown for qualities; shape, color, duration, and bigness. I have told the class that much in their future will depend on their ability to blow bubbles out of the information they have been presented. They must learn to blow bubbles on paper. If that means Scantron tests ad nauseam and thirty vocabulary words a week, so be it. They are to understand that everyone sees learning in different ways; some as a thing quantifiable, machine read and scored, others as amorphous and vague as a bubble set free to float on air. Today for me they blow bubbles; tomorrow they are yours."

The students enter with nervous chatter as they see their former teacher in the back of the room. Mr. Moderno addresses the class, "Please be seated and give me your attention for a moment. As you can see, Mrs. Kiljoy has returned and has missed all of you. Please say hello to her." Mr. Moderno pauses while various welcomes and hellos are shouted. "She has come in today to listen to your final exams and see how much you have progressed so that after the semester break she will be able to pick right up where we finish. We have had a good meeting and I am trusting you to be on your best behavior under her guidance. As you remember, yesterday I asked you to think of one statement that you wished to share with all of us. One idea to include in the bubble you will set free to float. When you are ready, stand up and blow your bubble. Then state your idea, shout it, or sing it over and over. Say it in English or Spanish, or whisper it if you want. Just make it count. Follow your bubble as it crosses the room and meets other bubbles or explodes. After your bubble breaks, sit down and listen to the ideas. Listen to each other."

He pauses. "Who will begin?"

The first child stands up. Mr. Moderno hands her the bucket. She is a beautiful brown girl with braided hair. She carefully holds the plastic wand, raises it to pursed lips, and sets a bubble off— perfectly. She turns to look at Mr. Moderno, then at Mrs. Kiljoy, then at the class. In a clear voice she sings out, "Education is a right, not a privilege." ❖

A VIEW FROM

RELIGION

RELIGIOUS PLURALISM

– LISA KEMMERER

R eligious pluralism is a fact in the United States; it is also a possibility. No longer considered a Protestant country, the United States is now home to a multitude of religious faiths and movements. Today there are more Muslims in the U.S. than Episcopalians. In 1993, a resident of Pittsburgh might watch a Hindu procession pass by the synagogue, or a Buddhist monk cross the street in front of a local mosque. We can attend a Southern Baptist church in Idaho or do Zen meditation in Massachusetts. Islamic schools, Sikh festivals, Hindu temples, and Jain summer camps are all part of the American landscape.

In the past thirty years, especially due to the Immigration Act of 1965, this landscape has changed significantly. Many of these faiths have come to live in the same communities, as neighbors, although not always peacefully. In this new environment, religious pluralism is a reality that affects the lives of all citizens, whether deeply religious or atheistic; accordingly, each of us must become aware of the face that this new pluralistic society wears.

The Pluralism Project, spearheaded by Diana Eck at Harvard, records a 1990 census report that calculates an increase of the Asian population in Minnesota at 194 percent, in Georgia at 208 percent, and in Rhode Island a whopping 245 percent. In the past ten years the Asian population of Boston has doubled, a statistic borne out by the census records: whereas fewer than 2,000 South Asian immigrants came to the U.S. in the entire decade of the 1950s, over 22,000 arrived in 1980 alone.

How are we to understand the concept and the practice of faith in this remarkably pluralistic nation? How has this new religious pluralism affected social and philosophical issues in the United States? What will be its effects on all of us in the future? These are some of the questions that must direct the forming of a vision of the future.

Lisa Kemmerer is a graduate student at Harvard Divinity School. She is studying world religions and is interested in teaching comparative religion. Lisa holds an undergraduate degree from Reed College in international studies. She is an active defender of animal rights and the conservation of nature.

THE REPROACH OF PATRIARCHY

The book *After Patriarchy: Feminist Transformations of the World Religious* offers a collection of essays written by women from within the Apache, Hindu, Buddhist, Jewish, Christian, and Islamic religious traditions. *After Patriarchy* presents a cross-cultural view of the problem of male domination in established religious traditions. This new publication demonstrates religious pluralism in action. No single faith is recognized as the exclusive holder of truth. Each faith is placed on an equal basis with all others. The scholars who compiled *After Patriarchy* understood that each of us can benefit from the religious diversity around us and that it is important for us to do so. In particular, religious diversity can offer a broader perspective on the complex problem of patriarchy.

Speaking of Faith, edited by Diana Eck and Devaki Jain in 1987, is a collection of essays written by women from an even greater variety of nations and faiths in an attempt to shed light on women, religion, and social change from a pluralistic perspective. The assumption underlying the collection is clear: each tradition can benefit from the accumulative knowledge of all the other traditions. Furthermore, these arguments make us aware of the opportunities that diversity offers by if we recognize each faith as an equally valid system of beliefs. The exclusionists' argument, which loudly asserts that "We are right, you are wrong," has been a primary feature of Western culture for centuries, characterized chiefly by male dominance. The Christian tradition of "Father, Son, and Holy Ghost" has been interpreted in the light of this patriarchal suppression and exclusion of women. Under the new pluralism, however, both men and women will become aware of the opportunities offered by this religious diversity, and those who disagree with the exclusionists' point of view will feel less isolated. Indeed, they will see that religious pluralism offers a multitude of choices and ways of assessing and understanding the major conflicts and problems that lie deep within most religious traditions of the world.

In *All Religions Are True,* Gandhi states that faith is like a spouse: one is sufficient for a lifetime, but it represents only a single, imperfect possibility. He therefore encourages each person to examine his or her own religious tradition in order to identify those aspects that represent truth. He encourages us to reconsider aspects of our faith that do not represent truth, and to learn from the faiths of others. The criterion Gandhi presents for determining "truth" is *ahimsa* or nonviolence: anything that results in harm to living beings, whether human or animal, cannot be considered truth.

FUTURE EFFECTS OF THE NEW PLURALISM

How will this new outlook, brought on by religious pluralism, affect our futures? Religious pluralism allows each of us a greater chance for spiritual fulfillment. The pluralistic approach insists on religious commitment. Only through our own faith can we come to understand the faiths of our neighbors. The pluralistic approach is a commitment to promote religious diversity and to respect differences between our faith and that of our neighbors. Pluralism offers an effective approach to a religiously diverse national citizenship, encouraging each of us to have faith, to examine our own beliefs critically, and to engage in dialogue with others. Through dialogue we must individually discover the truth that each religion offers. Pluralism asks each of us to view our own faith as part of a larger human spirituality, one that sees all other traditions as viable parts of this collective human expression. Just as learning Spanish helps us to understand English better, exploring Hinduism or Manichaeism can help Christians and Jews to understand their spirituality more deeply. As religious beings, whether we identify ourselves with a particular institution or not, we can learn from each human attempt to comprehend the divine. Renegotiation of religious terms allows us to communicate across traditions. People of one religious faith can interact with those of another in order that both can better understand the nature of religious commitment and the human experience of spirituality.

Religious pluralism is now an irreversible reality in the United States. We can no longer talk of "us" and "them," or refer to Hindus as if they existed only in Asia. The presence of a multitude of religions and religious groups in one country allows all of us a greater chance for spiritual fulfillment. We need not remain in a tradition that does not satisfy our spiritual needs. If we do not like the tradition in which we are reared, we have a variety of others that may be more compatible with our needs. Women and men, for example, who do not support male-dominated religious institutions can seek a faith that does address their spiritual needs, or they can incorporate ideas and practices from other faiths to create a spirituality that is more suitable. Our spiritual affiliations will be increasingly informed by a variety of faiths, which will be even more visibly and strongly represented in our communities in years to come. The acceptance of all faiths on equal footing will allow for the free growth and expansion of non-Western religious traditions. Pluralism will result in an even healthier religious diversity. This assortment of religious alternatives will encourage the reformation of dominant faiths.

Through increasing the diversity of religious responses and faiths, pluralism will continue to present viable alternatives to

traditional attitudes and social positions. Many of these alternatives will provide pressure for social change. Such is the challenge
that religious pluralism presents to traditional attitudes toward
homosexuality, the position of women within the church, or the
uses and misuses of non-human animals and the environment. In
response to the challenges of other faiths, more women will be
ordained in the Christian churches, and many homophobic religious institutions will remove or even reverse their policies. In the
next decade the pressures of religious pluralism will help bring
oppressed groups such as women and homosexuals to positions of
respected leadership in Western religious traditions.

We will also see changes in attitudes toward socio-political
issues. Ideas such as Gandhi's *ahimsa* are relevant to protection of
non-human animal life, the struggle against capital punishment,
peace movements, and the efforts of environmentalists to protect
the earth. In this next decade these influences will continue to
spread. We will see pluralism put to work to change aspects of our
lives which do not fit our expanding spiritual outlook. More
students will refuse to dissect frogs; more people will turn to
vegetarianism; more hunters will be questioned about their choice
of "sport." There will be less talk about the "Muslim world" as if it
were somewhere far removed from this country, and more people
will come to see that the United States is part of the Muslim world.
As a result, wars with "other" people—those who profess a different faith—will become more difficult to justify. We will find it
much harder to send our religiously plural military off to fight wars
in "foreign" countries.

The increased influence from this greater diversity of religious
expressions will affect our understanding of many important
issues, and the role of religion in our daily lives. For example,
Liberation Theology, an expression of Christianity developed in
South America, has brought a powerful new Biblical interpreta-
tion to the United States, which has strengthened the voices of
oppressed citizens like women and African-Americans. Liberation
Theology has presented a new force challenging the established
church.

Expanding religious pluralism will affect every community in
fundamental ways. The study of comparative religions will become
part of our standard public school curriculum, and instructors will
need to work with precision and sensitivity because the students in
the classfroom will belong to a variety of religious traditions. Some
aspects of Islamic law will find a place in the United States legal
system, and the complexities of the customs of so many different
faiths will have far-reaching effects on our laws. For instance, a Sikh
who recently objected to a hard-hat requirement because it pre-

vented the use of the customary Sikh turban must be accommo-
dated. We will see many more articles in the newspaper dealing
with people of various faiths who are asking that laws be adjusted
to recognize their particular needs in our pluralistic nation.

The multitude of religious traditions in the United States will
offer much more breadth and color to our collective arts and
language. Words like *ahimsa, dharma, salat, sangha,* and scores of
others will become as familiar to us as nirvana and karma have
become in the past decade.

In the near future, religious pluralism will be an even greater
catalyst for changes affecting every aspect of our collective culture.
The diversity of faiths in the United States offers breadth and
depth to our collective culture. It is happening, it will continue to
happen, and it is good *karma.* ❖

A VIEW FROM

DESIGN

EXOTIC TERRAINS:
AN ARCHITECTURE FOR THE LANDSCAPE OF THE FUTURE

– KRISTINA HILL

THE VISION

There's a mist shifting over the valley as you walk the outer edge of your community's land. Last night was the night of renewal, when bonfires are built to consume the winter's dead wood and a parade of fire-watchers march the flames out from their origins to refresh the grasslands. Looking out over the russet-tinged marshes, which were restored to change waste waters into fresh water, you notice the CenterRail train on its elevated track. The bright metal station house stretches across two wide strips of pavement, gray ribbons twisting off toward the horizon which were once roads. The train's whistle sounds once, sending a flock of cranes up from the wetlands to scatter the mists with a thousand pairs of white wings.

THE DISCIPLINE OF DESIGN

The aim of many academic disciplines is to extend the boundaries of the known world, pushing back the territory of mystery one discovery at a time. In the sciences, theories succeed by explaining as many mysteries as possible. Whole generations of students are given the impression that much about the world has been explained and that their task will be to fill in the remaining conspicuous gaps. Design begins with a different idea. It begins with the necessity of re-inventing the wheel, where the "wheel" is a symbol for a relationship configured between the known and the unknown. It is not engaged in filling the "gaps" in our knowledge of the world. Instead, the discipline of design reconfigures what is "known" to create a central place for the much broader terrain and tectonics of mystery—a space for the "unknown."

Kristina Hill received her B.S. degree in Geology from Tufts University, studied at Tübingen and the Museum School of the Boston Museum of Fine Arts. After earning a Master's degree in Landscape Architecture, she taught for two years at Iowa State University, then returned to Harvard to begin work on her doctorate in Design with a focus on ecological restoration.

In the world of a designer, the world might still be flat, or it might be a double helix instead of a globe. There are no explicit bounds on vision, on point of view. The same rational assumptions that constrain and order the visions of other academic fields can be liabilities to creativity in design. In landscape architecture the borderland between "natural" and "artificial," which has been so tensely guarded in popular language, appears and disappears disarmingly. Urban parks designed and created on bare ground can seem "natural" a generation later, as is New York's Central Park or Boston's Fenway. It is this ability to conjure, to call forth and shape the development of recognizable landscapes but not to control their future in any precise way, which allows each designer to embody a particular worldview in a specific place. It is a synthetic discipline, drawing on the configurations of knowledge presented by ecology, geology, aesthetics, law, history, and economics—but not constrained by their rationales.

A Shape for Things to Come

The configuration of a culture's landscape has always conveyed something vital about that culture's understanding of its "place" in the larger world. It is a version of the chicken and the egg dilemma: does a culture learn its cosmology from its landscape, or create a landscape that reflects what it already believes? I would argue that the landscape both reflects and informs a contemporary worldview. But this mutual causal relationship is not constant over time, as I will show, and it is leading us to a new understanding today as we experience the "crisis" of our environment.

In American culture, and indeed to some extent in all urbanized culture, the links in this feedback communication have been weakened and distorted by our increasing disconnection from our landscapes. We increasingly think water comes from the tap, not lakes and rivers. That food comes from grocery stores, not gardens and slaughterhouses. That building materials come from the lumber store, not the forest. This urbanizing trend in which we become less and less cognizant of our resource base is not new; on the contrary, it dates back to the growth of our cities and international market economies in the seventeenth century. As we have gone further and further toward becoming an entirely urban and suburban population, our landscape has changed at an ever increasing rate. Whereas in the eighteenth and nineteenth centuries the grandeur of America's native landscapes seemed real and the cities seemed more like shantytowns growing overnight, today's situation is in many ways reversed. Our cities and suburbs seem like "reality" while wilderness areas and wildlife habitats shrink to fragments apparently overnight.

How is our American cosmology reflected in these changes, embodied within our national landscape? This is the designer's central question, the question that will shape the architecture of our future.

I had a conversation recently with a Lakota man who raises wolves and buffalo on the Cheyenne River Sioux Reservation in South Dakota. We remarked on the way in which the fear of animals as "wildlife" has disappeared from urban areas like New York City, only to be replaced by the dread of new urban "wolves" in the shape of human beings. Maybe human culture becomes, in a way, what it has replaced. In a wilderness landscape, the town is a haven for human similarity in the face of unknown dangers. In a completely urbanized context, we realize that we are in fact afraid of each other, of ourselves—that wilderness exists within humans as well as without. Indeed, our cosmology reflects a journey into ourselves, into a landscape that is formed by what we have up to now called "the artificial" or "man-made" world.

Our technology has begun to focus on mimicking life. Biotechnology tries to direct evolution from within the genetic code of an organism; artificial intelligence systems have begun to share significant borders with system games that mimic a kind of disembodied life in "virtual reality" or "cyberspace." Our cosmology is on a rollercoaster ride into the human psyche as an analog for all life, even as our urban expansion and industrial agriculture eliminate much of the diversity of other life forms. We are well on the way to becoming the wilderness in our world.

DESIGNING IN A NEW WILDERNESS

Much of the commentary on environmental change over the last twenty years has sounded an apocalyptic note, loudly and insistently. This clarion has combined two messages, one a call to action and the other, somewhat paradoxically, that it is already too late to halt many of the changes we have set in motion. A smaller group has championed the optimism of technology, maintaining that we will continue to invent and innovate our way out of environmental apocalypse. Most of our technological response so far, however, has been far too little and too late to compensate for the scale of changes predicted for the atmosphere, for example, or for the loss of tropical rainforests.

From the point of view of design, we are consuming our way out of our traditional worldview, much as a chick consumes the inside of its egg before it hatches. The socio-environmental connection is catching up with us, penetrating our sleepwalking with its warning messages. But what can emerge now from the egg, as we find our environment changed forever? There is a threshold that we must cross and that the discipline of design must help us cross, between an old body and a new body. By its ability to re-embody our worldview in landscapes, landscape architecture must build the bridges to a new nature that includes human life as a member, not as a self-absorbed consumer.

We human beings must emerge into a new role and take our place among others of the so-called habitat re-forming taxa in nature. There are wetlands to restore, woodlands to tend and grow, waters to be cleaned, social inequities to be compensated— all labors that can be accomplished with our own physical energies and some of our simplest technological partnerships with other forms of life. Soil microorganisms have been cultured for use in everything from breaking down metal car bodies to cleaning up oil spills and landfill contaminants. A recent Norwegian study documented the presence of 4,000 to 5,000 different microorganisms in just a gram of soil, whose ecological potential we do not yet understand or appreciate. The species of living creatures that survive the changes of our environment will be our partners in re-forming our habitat, and designers of landscapes will re-embody this knowledge in the configuration of those habitats to continue the cycle of feedback. We will build landscapes that embody the flows of energy, organisms, and materials so that we can understand the infrastructures we genuinely depend upon. Through design, we can communicate with each other about these changes and adapt to them at the same time.

There has been a tendency in our creation of technology to seek an escape from our bodies. Much of this, I would argue, is due to the psycho-social development of those who create the technologies. There is an urgent need in our new technologies and designs to incorporate the insight of other social groups. We must put the distinctly embodied concerns of women, racial minorities, and elder humans into the development of our technology and designs, seeing ourselves as strongest when we are diverse. Otherwise, we will continue to be trapped by the youthful illusion of immortality, by masculinist supremacy, and by post-adolescent fears of communal identity. Landscape architecture can and must offer a re-centered vision that responds to embodied persons, not rational ideals. Partnerships with other life forms in low-technology resource systems, based in the expenditure of human labor and other renewable energies, are "appropriate technologies."

Exotic Terrains

There is no turning back from the future. It is coming whether we want it to or not, and it looks likely to bring major changes with it. It need not, however, be perceived as an apocalypse.

The current status of landscape architecture as a relatively minor player makes it seem an improbable source of adaptive solutions. Yet the ability to re-form our culture's worldview and embody that renewed vision in our landscapes is undeniably critical to our future. Each of us can participate in this effort to redesign human landscapes. Local design action and regional planning are the critical links to adaptation in a new global context. The next century of changes will require us to re-form our habitats and our understanding of ourselves. It will happen most poignantly to our children and grandchildren, but it must begin with us. ❖

A VIEW FROM

HISTORY

WRITING A NEW CHAPTER
IN THE HISTORY OF
INTERNATIONAL RELATIONS

– ANDREW P. N. ERDMANN

On 21 November 1990 President George Bush told the delegates gathered at the Conference on Security and Cooperation in Europe (CSCE) for the signing of the Charter of Paris for a New Europe that "the Cold War is over." The Charter and a new treaty limiting conventional forces in Europe signed by the CSCE's thirty-four member states—the United States, Canada, and all the nations of Europe (except Albania)—codified that Europe was no longer divided between two hostile alliances. With the signing of these accords, President Bush concluded that "we have closed a chapter of history."

The Cold War chapter of the history of international relations may be closed, but what the next one will contain is far from clear. For the first time since the onset of the Cold War in the late 1940s, restructuring the international order seems a realistic possibility. After experiencing the Gulf War, the disintegration of the Soviet Union, and a modern Russian revolution in less than three years, we can safely conclude that things are changing. But beyond this truism, can we foretell what international relations will be like at the turn of the century?

Since historians trade in the past, not the future, they can apparently offer little to the answering of this question. Such an

Andrew P. N. Erdmann is a Ph.D. candidate in American History and a Mellon Fellow in the Humanities. Before coming to Harvard, he received a B.A. degree in history and political science from Williams College in 1988 and a second B.A. in philosophy, politics, and economics from Oxford University in 1990. Under the guidance of Professors Akira Iriye and Ernest May, he is currently beginning his dissertation on the evolution of Americans' conceptions of "victory" during the twentieth century. He wishes to acknowledge the profound impact that these advisers have had on his understanding of international history.

impression would be mistaken, however. Although the Cold War's last page may have been written, much of its plot, central themes, and even some of its characters will continue to shape the next chapter in the history of international relations. In many respects, therefore, these pages will reflect the revision of the old world order as much as the creation of a new one. In lieu of predictions, historical analysis can offer something less ambitious but nevertheless more realistic: it can identify some of the fundamental influences that will be carried over into this new era of international relations from the old and then suggest how they might plausibly interact in the years ahead.

The Cold War has bequeathed to us much that will influence our future. Two examples from today's headlines prove this point. First, the prospects of long-term social and economic dislocations will confront nations ranging from the former Soviet Union to the United States as entire sections of the world economy are converted from military to civilian uses. Second, years of superpower sponsored arms build-ups throughout the world will continue to exacerbate regional instabilities as evidenced most poignantly in the chaos and armed banditry of Somalia.

Historical analysis, however, can advance our understanding of future conflicts beyond merely listing such manifest legacies of the Cold War. Historical analysis can expose deeper, less obvious, yet perhaps more fundamental themes of the Cold War era that will structure the future narrative of the international relations. This essay, therefore, will focus upon two of our key inheritances from the Cold War—new ideas about the nature of international relations and existing institutions—and then sketch the possible outcomes of their interaction in the decade ahead.

The Cold War era has given us new understandings about the dynamics of international relations. Specifically, it fostered a greater appreciation of the role that shared interest plays in the affairs between states. At first blush, this appears to present a paradox: was not the Cold War essentially a confrontation between two irreconcilably hostile, ideological blocs, not a quest for international cooperation?

This paradox is dispelled, however, once one recognizes that it was exactly this clash between two powerful alliances that fostered the growth of new conceptions of shared or transnational interest in international relations. In the aftermath of the Second World War, the nations of Europe faced the enormous task of reconstruction. Initially many hoped that the wartime alliance of the Great Britain, France, the United States, and the Soviet Union would continue to function as both the guarantor of peace through the new United Nations and the framework for economic reconstruction. Ideological tensions, mutual misunderstandings, and genuine differences in conceptions of security, however, quickly drove a wedge between these allies. By the late 1940s the Cold War had begun: East and West then confronted mutual military fear and the burdens of reconstruction.

In this soil of distrust, fear, and weakness, the seeds of international cooperation began to spread roots and bear fruit. Western European and American leaders recognized that the tasks of economic rejuvenation and deterring future military aggression in Europe could never be achieved by nations pursuing unilateral policies. This awareness of transnational interest began to integrate Western nations as never before. First, the United States pursued the revitalization of the international economy through the Marshall Plan. Then in 1949 the United States, Canada, and the nations of Western Europe took the unprecedented step of forming the North Atlantic Treaty Organization (NATO), an alliance which equated a military attack on any member as an attack on all. In the following decade the Western European nations themselves took their first substantive steps toward economic and political union—steps ranging from the creation of the European Court of Human Rights in 1949 to the formation of the European Economic Community with the Treaty of Rome in 1957. These initiatives have endured and, in the case of European economic and political integration, developed further until the end of the Cold War.

If the Cold War left us only NATO and European efforts toward integration, it would hardly have given us "new understandings about the dynamics of international relations" as claimed above. After all, the notion of alliances for common defense has existed as long as the history of warfare, and the belief that an open international economic order has long-term benefits for all of its participants can be traced back at least as far as Adam Smith.

The experience of the Cold War, however, pushed statesmen and scholars alike to conclude that common interest lies at the heart of relations between international adversaries just as it does between allies. This novel conclusion arose from the historically unique power possessed by the East and West during the Cold War. Even if only conventional weapons were used, a military confrontation between NATO and the Soviet Union's Warsaw Pact alliance could have eclipsed the destruction of the Second World War, which claimed the lives of over 50 million people. More importantly, the destructive capacity of nuclear weapons—which both sides possessed in frightening numbers by the end of the 1950s—presented for the first time in the history of international relations the realistic threat that no one, not even neutral states, would even *survive* a major war. This interest in survival was mutual and by necessity transcended other disputes.

Starting in the late 1950s, this new understanding that even the fiercest of international competitors shared real, transnational interests generated a new wave of scholarship and policy initiatives. The importation of formal mathematical models from the study of microeconomics to the study of international relations by game theorists like Harvard's Thomas Schelling was the most famous and important of these developments. Placing at the center of their analyses the interdependence of interests, these models helped inform the United States government's and the American people's acceptance by the 1960s of the idea that mutual vulnerability to nuclear attack would help secure international stability: no nation would ever launch an attack if its own destruction was guaranteed by retaliation. These ideas of interdependence and mutual interest, in turn, crucially shaped the progress of arms control to the present day.

The implications of this new conceptualization of international politics as a game with both competitive *and* cooperative elements were then felt well beyond the narrow confines of arms control and national security issues. Trying to conceive of how cooperative arrangements could be instituted, either formally or informally, led to the investigation of what political scientists call "regimes"—the norms, procedures, and rules upon which these arrangements are based. More recently, the crucial role played by experts from different nations who, sharing a certain vision of an international problem, cooperate to define transnational interests has been recognized in the growing literature under the cumbersome rubric of "epistemic communities." Such studies have revealed increasingly self-conscious efforts by governments and international organizations to address transnational interests such as nuclear non-proliferation, economic cooperation, environmental protection, and scientific collaboration.

The shared experience of trying to prevent the Cold War from escalating into a mutually destructive hot war generated a new vision of international relations. This new awareness of transnational interests will continue to shape international affairs in the years ahead.

The pages of the next chapter in the history of international relations, however, will not be filled with descriptions of the unchecked progress of efforts to create a more cooperative and interdependent international system because of other inheritances from the Cold War era. A variety of institutions that either endured through the Cold War from earlier eras or were created to cope with the exigencies of the superpower confrontation are ill-suited to securing transnational interests and yet will continue to shape international relations.

The most important of these institutional impediments to the pursuit of transnational interests is the nation state itself. Despite the dreams of world federalists and the growing awareness of transnational interests, the international system is still dominated by individual states over whom exists no superior sovereign authority. Every nation state's supreme objective is to secure its own individual interests by any means judged prudent. And this defining feature of the nation state will work against international cooperation on two levels—the level of international organizations and the level of domestic support for transnational policies.

First, all nation states have shared, and will continue to share, an aversion to granting any of their sovereignty to an international organization that could then use this power to pursue transnational interests at the expense of their narrowly defined national interest. This fear has shaped all international institutions. For example, the founders of the United Nations predicated it upon the belief that the preservation of national sovereignty should be its guiding purpose. The current cases of cold feet throughout Europe concerning the Maastricht Treaty's plans for a more unified economic and monetary system highlight that such sentiments still influence policy.

Second, despite the recent fragmentation of the multi-ethnic states of the Soviet Union and Yugoslavia, the nation state remains the focus of most individuals' allegiance in international affairs. This loyalty is deeply embedded in notions of shared historical identity, ethnic pride and prejudice, and group solidarity. Accordingly, domestic support for foreign policies that pursue an easily recognizable interest of the state is usually more forthcoming than for more general transnational interests. Especially during phases of cyclical economic downturn and domestic retrenchment, the general public may not support any foreign policy initiative. The American public's current negative opinion of further aid to the Russian Republic exemplifies this reality.

Nation states have endured as the fundamental actors in international affairs for centuries. In the twentieth century even the dreadful experiences of two world wars did not force these states to accept a superior sovereign authority. The force of transnational interests could scarcely be expected to be more persuasive than the deaths of millions. There is, therefore, no prospect on the horizon that nation states will be transcended in the immediate future.

While perhaps not as serious an impediment to international cooperation as the nation state itself, other institutions, both governmental and international, inherited from the Cold War era have demonstrated that they cannot address the full range of transnational concerns that already demand attention. Because the prevention of another world war remained the preeminent priority throughout the Cold War era, more concern and resources were devoted to those institutions that dealt directly with military and security matters than to those associated with other international concerns. The experience of the United States during the Cold War, though relatively extreme, is nonetheless representative of these trends. Within the United States the newly formed intelligence community and unprecedented peacetime military apparatus commanded the lion's share of the budget for foreign affairs; organizations such as the Agency for International Development were correspondingly neglected. Similarly, with the onset of the Cold War the Soviet Union's possession of the veto in the Security Council meant that the United Nations could never be the primary international body through which the United States sought to preserve its security; accordingly, the United Nations became a speaker's forum while the United States shifted its energies to NATO. In sum, the military nature of the Cold War caused uneven institutional evolution throughout the world.

International developments since President Bush's proclamation of the end of the Cold War highlight the relative strengths and weaknesses of these inherited institutions. As the Gulf War demonstrated, these bodies can adequately cope with crises cast in the mold of traditional military aggression by one state against another's sovereignty. The governments of the West coordinated their response to the invasion of Kuwait in a timely fashion, deploying and sustaining military forces in an inhospitable climate. Because the Iraqi violation of Kuwaiti sovereignty was so flagrant, the United Nations functioned as it was originally designed, thus supplying the legal bases for the use of force against Iraq. Though some questions remain about the proper role of Congress in the American decision to resort to force, the American national security apparatus performed competently if not well throughout the crisis. The case of Somalia reaffirms that if an acceptable military solution to a crisis can be found, existing institutions can eventually respond. Where no quick military solution is possible, however, serious transnational interests tend to be neglected. The United Nations, NATO, the Organization of American States, and the Organization of Africa Unity, as well as individual nations, have all demonstrated their inability to conceive of solutions to the problem of refugees from Yugoslavia, Haiti, Liberia, and Vietnam, to name only a few countries of conflict. Plans to ameliorate the reasons for the refugees' flight, usually ethnic and civil strife, have proved even more elusive. Similarly, despite the Rio Summit's initial promise, little has been accomplished in the sphere of international environmental regulation. The chronic problem of Third World underdevelopment defies the efforts of institutions like the World Bank. Moreover, serious health issues, including population control and the spread of infectious diseases like

AIDS, still lack a global strategy.

With the end of the Cold War, the most serious threat to every nation's security—the possibility of a nuclear world war—has receded. Traditional military threats will continue to exist, but many of the institutions designed for the Cold War can meet these challenges. The diminishing of traditional military threats, however, throws into stark relief existing institutions' deficiencies in dealing with transnational interests like the environment, refugee policy, ethnic unrest, and economic development. Existing institutions and norms will need to be revised or replaced, if these concerns are to be addressed during the next decade.

A set of profoundly conflicted themes, therefore, emerge from the Cold War chapter of our history. The enormous peril posed by the prospect of another world war promoted a new understanding of international relations that emphasized cooperation, even between adversaries, in order to secure transnational interests. The grounding of the international system in the nation state, however, continues to encourage policies rooted in narrow national interest. Between these centripetal and centrifugal forces, inherited governmental bodies and international institutions should cope adequately with military threats analogous to those they were originally designed to confront during the Cold War; yet they are currently ill-equipped to handle other increasingly salient transnational concerns.

Having identified these themes of continuity from the Cold War era, the question remains of how they will interact to shape international relations as the end of the millennium approaches. While it is always too soon for historical analysis to predict the future, the interplay of these themes delimits five possible futures for international relations, covering the spectrum from the undesirable to desirable.

The least desirable future would be the reemergence of a serious military threat to international stability which thrusts the world back into another Cold War. International cooperation on transnational interests other than those tied to security concerns would languish. A rejuvenated, ultra-nationalist Russia, armed with its nuclear arsenal, is the only plausible candidate for the role of military menace in the next decade. In its fractious political and weakened economic condition, however, this is the least likely of the five possible futures.

The disintegration of the international community into regional blocs, dominated by unilateral policies and neglect of transnational interests, is the next possible future. Some of the rhetoric in the 1992 presidential campaign echoed calls in the past for a Fortress America approach to the world. More seriously, the first shots in potential trade wars between the United States and

the European Community and Japan have already been fired. Continued slow global economic growth could exacerbate these tensions further. Though slightly more desirable than a sequel to the Cold War, this future is imminently more possible.

Just "muddling through" is the most likely future. Continuing along our current trajectory, in this scenario the tensions between transnational interests and nation states are addressed on an ad hoc, crisis management basis. Dominated by bureaucratic inertia and reactive policies, this future will contain some success in international cooperation as well as many failures because responses, if forthcoming, will often be too late.

In the fourth future, elites and technocrats throughout the world work toward greater international cooperation through channels obscured from public scrutiny. The strength of the approach to international cooperation is also its fundamental weakness. Sheltered from the vicissitudes of public opinion, new agreements could be formulated based upon an international consensus of experts. However, these same agreements would be very vulnerable in the long-term because changes in the international or economic climate would almost certainly lead to some public questioning of their basis. Even beneficial accords might then be unwittingly scuttled as political leaders respond to public demands for immediate action.

The fifth future is the most desirable. As in the fourth future, elites throughout the world work together to define new institutions and norms for international relations. In this scenario, however, these same elites promote the legitimation of the new order by actively seeking public understanding and support. The new order, with its broader conceptions of national interest, would become embedded in the body politic of individual nations. Ultimately, this new conception of national interest would remove some of the impediments to the realization of transnational interests that the current narrow nation state perspective creates. Stability, proactive cooperation, and widespread understanding of and support for international initiatives would characterize this future. While the most desirable of the five potential futures, this vision would undoubtedly be the most difficult to realize. A sustained and dedicated effort by the governments of the world to create such an order, while incorporating their citizens as partners in the process, would be a prerequisite for success.

The historian of today cannot predict which one of these possibilities will follow the Cold War chapter in a future history of international relations. That is a story for a historian of the next millennium to chronicle. The chapter that this future historian writes, however, will be an account of the choices that we will make in the years ahead. ❖